England's Ghostly Heritage

Also by Terence Whitaker:

Lancashire's Ghosts and Legends
Yorkshire's Ghosts and Legends
Dr Ruxton of Lancaster
Ghosts of Old England (US title *Haunted England*)
North Country Ghosts and Legends
Play:
He'll Have To Go, Mrs Lovejoy

England's Ghostly Heritage

TERENCE WHITAKER

ROBERT HALE · LONDON

© *Terence Whitaker 1989*
First published in Great Britain 1989

Robert Hale Limited
Clerkenwell House
Clerkenwell Green
London EC1R 0HT

British Library Cataloguing in Publication Data

Whitaker, Terence W.
  England's ghostly heritage
  1. England. Ghosts. History
  I. Title
  133.1'0942

ISBN 0-7090-3700-7

Photoset in North Wales by
Derek Doyle & Associates, Mold, Clwyd.
Printed in Great Britain by
St Edmundsbury Press Ltd, Bury St Edmunds, Suffolk.
Bound by WBC Bookbinders Limited.

Contents

Dedicated to my friend and confidant
Dr S.S. Raza
without whose help and support
none of this would have been
possible.

Illustrations

Haunted Houses

PICTURE CREDITS

Author's collection: 1-6, 10, 12, 15, 17, 19-21. Madame Tussauds, London: 4-5. James Roads: 7-9, 11, 13-14. Netherhall School: 16. Michelle Temple: 18.

Preface

Interest in ghosts and the paranormal has increased tremendously over the past decade. Perhaps this interest is a perfectly natural one, since most people regard ghosts either as an agreeable, thrilling or horrifying form of folk-lore or as a possible key to a genuine form of communication with those who have died. Whichever way one views them, ghost stories are part of the story-teller's magic which has fascinated humanity for untold centuries.

England is rich in ghost-lore, and even the smallest village claims some lingering traditional story of a haunted spot. Castles, manor houses, humble cottages, old inns, crossroads and rivers all have, or have had, their ghosts. Some are centuries old, but as they are still experienced today, ghosts do not seem to become out of date, and a modern council house or factory is as likely to be haunted as any ancient and crumbling fortress.

Just why the British Isles, and England in particular, should claim more ghosts than anywhere else, I have yet to discover. Perhaps now that we have lost our Empire and are no longer the most powerful nation in the world, we have nothing left to cling to but our traditions. Perhaps the supernatural has always been a subject that has evoked a special kind of inquisitiveness: a search for the knowledge that there may be a life beyond the grave. I do not expect through this book to determine the matter one way or another, but many of the events recorded are too well authenticated to be disregarded as the products of the overworked imagination of frightened people.

Some ghosts, it would appear, have a sense of humour, others are grim and malicious, and many appear to have no apparent reason to haunt a particular spot. Some of the stories are not very pleasant, dealing as they do with terrible violence, inhuman practices, jealousy, lust, violated promises and sudden death. Yet, at the same time, the events related have given rise to the macabre: tales of those long dead who cannot rest, unearthly scenes that have terrified the beholder, and strange happenings, many of which defy explanation.

Whether the reader is a sceptic or a believer in the supernatural, I hope these stories will help you think along the lines that not all supernatural phenomena are figments of the imagination, for if ghosts suffer from frustration, this must surely occur when they are seen but not recognized for what they are. It was C. Meadley, a fellow Yorkshireman, who wrote: 'It is the want of ghost-lore that makes colonies and new houses so bare of association. There is so much egotism in a place which belongs only to our own days. Talk of a lonely, ghost-like house! Why it is cheerful when compared with a lonely new one!'

I have been greatly surprised by the amount of interest shown in my book *Ghosts of Old England* and by the number of people who have written asking for more. So, for better or worse, here is another helping. As usual, I would remind the reader that most of the haunted sites mentioned are open to the public, but there are some which are private property, and I would ask you to respect that privacy.

Finally, I would like to acknowledge the help I have received from correspondents at home and abroad, far too numerous to mention by name: magazine and newspaper editors and the many librarians, for their co-operation extending over many years; James Roads, for taking several exceptionally good photographs at great inconvenience to himself; my wife Marjorie, for her inexhaustible patience, support and understanding, and all who have contributed in any way.

To all these lovely people, this book is dedicated with my sincere thanks.

Burnley, 1988	Terence Whitaker

'Science must either tabulate or ignore. Yet there must be great difficulty in tabulating ghosts, since the data of ghost stories can be tested by no instrument except the human mind, an instrument which varies in sensitiveness.'

Edith Oliver

1. The Criminal Ghosts of London

No one knew who he was or where he came from. He had stalked like a phantom through the gas-lit alleys and byways of the fog-enshrouded East End of Victorian London, and in just a few weeks in the autumn of 1888, his razor-sharp and lovingly honed knife had sliced deep through the tissue and gristle to unpick the very seams of the living bodies of five Whitechapel prostitutes. Then, suddenly and ghost-like, the creature simply vanished forever into the nothingness of time, leaving the sole chilling legacy of a name that still sets the flesh crawling one hundred years on – Jack the Ripper!

To this day there are people living in the East End who are convinced that Jack the Ripper has left a far more terrifying reminder of himself than just a name. He has, they are convinced, psychically stained the very air of his old killing-ground, and the ghosts of his pathetic victims may still be glimpsed from time to time, walking the streets as in life or slumped, ravaged, on the cobbles as at the time of their death, their cries re-echoing now and again, piercing the quietness of an East End night.

One of Britain's greatest ghost-hunters, Elliott O'Donnell, reported that about a month after the death of Elizabeth Stride – the Ripper's third victim – a respectable Whitechapel businessman was passing late one night through Berner Street, making his way to the Commercial Road when suddenly his hair was set bristling by a series of the most harrowing moans and groans. At first he thought the Ripper had struck again. A small crowd rapidly gathered but no one was able to pin-point the exact location of the blood-curdling noises.

According to O'Donnell, the businessman was just about to knock on the door of one of the houses when a woman in the crowd called out: 'It's no good knocking there, guv'nor. Them sounds don't come from there. They're in the street 'ere. We've often 'eard them since poor Lizzie was done to death!' Elizabeth Stride had been found in a yard beside No.40 Berner Street on 30 September 1888.

A few weeks earlier, on 13 August, the Ripper's first victim had been found in a gutter in Bucks Row in Whitechapel. She was Mary Ann Nichols. Her throat had been slashed almost from ear to ear and cut back to the vertebrae. Her windpipe and gullet had been severely slashed and there had also been extensive slashing and ripping of her abdomen.

There is very little left of Bucks Row today but, even so, on dark nights the area seems to have been caught in a time-warp, and a huddled figure is said to have been seen many times over the years, emitting a weird ghostly light. The spectre is usually seen lying just where Mary Ann Nichols was discovered in the gutter.

Jack the Ripper's second victim was Annie Chapman, whose disembowelled body was discovered in a yard behind No.29 Hanbury Street, Spitalfields, on 8 September 1888. Her throat had been cut with such savagery as almost to sever her head from her body. Annie's dreadful passing is said to be commemorated not only by the sounds of appalling groans and screams heard at night and obviously uttered by no living thing but, even worse, by the ghost of a headless woman seen night after night sitting on a wall near the scene of the crime.

The modern day ghost-hunter and President of the Ghost Club of Great Britain, author Peter Underwood, wrote as recently as 1973 that a huddled figure, thought to be the ghost of Catherine Eddowes, the Ripper's fourth victim, has been seen in a corner of Mitre Square in recent years. This is a spot long known to Londoners as 'Ripper's Corner'.

The last victim of Jack the Ripper was pretty Mary Kelly. She was found in a room at No.13 Millers Court in Spitalfields, the only victim to be discovered indoors. Her murderer had managed to reduce her to the contents of a butcher's offal tray, on 9 November 1888.

The tumbledown room in Millers Court where Mary was hacked to pieces and festooned about the peeling walls no longer exists, but as long as it stood it was always said to be haunted. Scores of East Enders said that the ghost of poor Mary, a woman in shabby black, was often seen entering the place and looking out of the dirt-glazed window.

When the British square-rigger *Pierrot* capsized in mid-Atlantic in July 1884, there were only four survivors. For over three weeks they huddled together in a battered lifeboat, slowly dying of exhaustion and starvation. One of the survivors was the ship's captain, Edward Rutt, and it was he who made the last, desperate suggestion that they should draw lots to determine which of them should be eaten, thus saving the lives of the others. Two of the seamen agreed, but the third, eighteen-year-old Richard Tomlin, the youngest member of the *Pierrot*'s crew, protested, saying that he would rather die than be involved with cannibalism. This reluctance sealed his fate, for at the first opportunity Captain Rutt crept towards the sleeping youngster and slit his throat.

The captain and the two remaining seamen had no qualms about eating their young shipmate and when, four days later, they were rescued by the yacht *Gellert*, it was the boy's flesh that had sustained them. However, the horror-stricken skipper of the *Gellert* rejected the idea of burying what was left of Richard Tomlin at sea and, hidden away under canvas, the body of the victim accompanied the three survivors into Falmouth.

Captain Rutt and the two seamen were charged, tried and condemned to death for murder on the high seas, but the then Home Secretary decided that there had been enough horror and, having closely examined the evidence and the unusual circumstances surrounding the case, he commuted the sentences to a mere six months imprisonment.

When the three men were released from gaol, they

faced a bleak future. No other shipowner would employ them and they were made outcasts, not only by their friends but by their families also. One of the seamen got a job as a drayman for a merchant in London. Two weeks after he had started the job, his team of horses saw something that frightened them in the middle of a foggy London street. Bolting, they threw the man to the ground, where he died after breaking his neck. Witnesses later testified that the 'thing' in the fog had been a figure swathed in bloodstained bandages – a figure which disappeared as soon as the man died.

Captain Rutt heard of the incident and went round the slums of the East End to seek out the other surviving seaman. He found him a sodden derelict in desperately bad health, far gone from the effects of too much gin. Rutt told him that some crazy relative out for revenge was posing as Richard Tomlin's ghost, and he urged the man to help ferret him out. But the old seaman only wanted more gin, and in a fit of DTs he was eventually taken to the charity ward of a London hospital where he died in a screaming, delirious fit. Eyewitnesses later said that another patient, 'dressed all in bandages', had been holding the man down, apparently trying to soothe him. Then the swathed patient vanished.

Captain Rutt was now in a state of abject terror. He went to the police, who scoffed at his tale of a fiend in bandages. However, in view of his apparent mental condition, they offered to allow him to spend the night in one of the police cells. Rutt went gratefully, checking the cell door several times to make sure he was still locked in.

As he had been accommodated in a cell block used for the disturbed, screams and cries in the night were not uncommon and often went unnoticed by the officers on duty. But when, at three o'clock in the morning, the police heard Rutt, his cries sent several officers running to his cell. They unlocked the door and went to Rutt's bunk, where he lay with his fingers scissored upwards and his eyes bulging and glazed like those of a dead fish. Clenched between his lifeless fingers, the shocked police officers saw shreds of cotton – and bloodstained gauze.

Another ghost of the criminous past is that of Mrs Amelia Elizabeth Dyer, the infamous baby-farmer. Her black bombazine wraith was seen in old Newgate Prison – a much-haunted place in its day.

The dank passages and ominous cells seemed to hold the musty vapour of generations of London fogs, something which cast a gloom over all who worked there. One old warder recorded: 'During the periods when the gallows were in requisition, the empty corridors were full of forms of fear. Death, dread and doom were in the air. The resonant hammering of the coffin makers was not a pleasant thing to hear, and the greasy hemp rope tackle hooked to the sinister beam in the execution shed was terrible to look upon.'

The chief warder at Newgate just prior to its demolition was a man called Scott. He was sensitive to atmosphere, little signs and symbols, disquieting trivia – and one thing, or person, who had an effect on him was Amelia Dyer, both alive and dead.

'It was not,' he later explained, 'that she was a troublesome prisoner, she was quite the reverse in fact, too oily and submissive for words. But her eyes were always watching me. Those glittering eyes of hers stilled into me a strange feeling of disquiet and foreboding. She was old and shrivelled and, as I watched her in the dock at the Old Bailey, I could not help wondering how old she was. I would not have been surprised to hear that she had looked the same for the last two hundred years!'

The keeper of Newgate Gaol had a black-and-white English setter dog which appeared to hate Mrs Dyer from the very first day it set eyes on her. It seemed to be affected by the faint, sickly reek which her body gave off and which reminded one warder of 'ancient marshlands under a strong sun'. The dog always cowered past her cell with its tail drawn in. In short, Amelia Dyer exuded all that was evil and corrupt.

On the day she was hanged, just before she walked out of her cell to go to the execution shed, Mrs Dyer looked over to Chief Warder Scott and said, 'I'll meet you again some day, sir.'

Mrs Dyer was hanged on 10 June 1896, and six years later Newgate Prison's doors clanged shut for the last time. One night, just before it closed, a group of warders were sharing a bottle of whisky to mark the final week of duty in the prison. They were gathered in the keeper's room, which was situated next to the old women felons' yard. They were able to see out into the yard through a small glass observation wicket in the door.

Suddenly Chief Warder Scott experienced a strong feeling that someone's eyes were fixed on him, and he heard a voice ringing in his head: 'Meet you again … meet you again sometime, sir.' There was something oddly familiar about the voice which sent images racing down his memory corridor. Dim, out-of-focus images. He could not put a face to the voice.

Then, glancing towards the yard door, he saw a face framed in the grill. There was no mistaking the oily, benevolent smile, the dark little snake-like eyes and the thin lips trying to look kind and harmless. It was Mrs Dyer – dead for over six years. She gave him one sad, enigmatic look and then faded slowly out of his vision. Scott and another warder jumped up and ran to the door, flinging it open. The yard was empty – except for a woman's handkerchief which fluttered to their feet on the wet flagstones. At that time there was not a single woman convict in the prison, nor had there been for over two years.

The uneasy shade of the evil old baby-farmer made one more recorded appearance. In the last week before Newgate shut its massive gates forever, a press photographer came to take pictures of the place for the record, and to photograph some of the officials. A photograph was taken of Chief Warder Scott standing with a colleague outside the execution shed. When the picture was developed, there was a woman's face looking over Scott's shoulder. He recognized her instantly – it was Mrs Dyer.

George Gaffney was a petty thief who operated in London's seedy red-light district of Soho at the turn of the century. His crimes were usually of a minor nature:

shoplifting, breaking and entering, petty larceny. Then, on 1 March 1910, things suddenly took a new turn.

Walking through Soho, Gaffney saw on a street-seller's cart a strange three-foot length of woven silk rope which he recognized as a 'thuggee cord' used by the Hindu assassin sect to despatch their victims. Gaffney bought it – and two weeks later he used it.

He had been having problems with a girl called Bessie Graves, who was pestering him to marry her because she was pregnant. But Gaffney had other ideas. He had wooed her under the alias of Arthur Eames, and now he wanted to discard her, because he had found a much more promising opportunity in the form of an elderly rich widow by the name of Stella Fortney.

On 17 March an hysterical landlady called the police, and Scotland Yard detectives sent to the scene discovered Bessie Graves dead, with the strangler's cord drawn so tightly around her throat that it was embedded in the flesh. Their only clue was that the probable strangler was a man who called himself Arthur Eames. There was little else for the police to go on, and three weeks later Gaffney was still at large, pursuing his romance with the rich widow.

One night it occurred to Gaffney that he would perhaps make a better impression on the widow if he was to call on her in a hansom cab. Minutes after hailing one he was screaming in terror, for in the half-light of the closed vehicle he had found the spectre of Bessie Graves sharing the seat with him. Her eyes stared glassily into his, her swollen tongue lolled obscenely from the side of her contorted mouth.

For well over a week after the incident, George Gaffney went on the bottle in one tremendous bender, in an attempt to drown out the vision of Bessie. Sobering up again, he then went to see Stella Fortney – who was, it appears, far from friendly towards him at first. But she soon melted when Gaffney gave her a diamond ring, unaware that he had stolen it earlier that day.

After they had shared a bottle of champagne, Stella asked Gaffney if he would go down into the cellar for another bottle. Bearing an oil lamp, he was half-way down the cellar steps when the spectre of Bessie Graves loomed out of the darkness to greet him. She had succeeded in loosening the strangler's cord, which hung round her throat like a necklace. Now the staring eyes were more terrifying than ever. Screaming, Gaffney threw the lamp at the figure and he crashed headlong down the steps to lie unconscious at the bottom.

Gaffney spent the next three weeks in hospital, and when he was discharged he decided that he had only one chance of throwing off the ghost which would never leave him alone. Perhaps, if he put England behind him forever, Bessie Graves would remain there. He booked passage on the liner *Montrose* for Quebec – the same liner that was to feature so dramatically in the arrest of Dr Crippen.

With renewed hope Gaffney checked into a small hotel on the eve of his voyage. Then, in the semi-gloom of his room, he saw Bessie's ghost again. This time she had freed herself of the silken noose and was holding it out to him. Feebly he took it from her claw-like hands and stared at it in horror. When he at last looked up again, Bessie had vanished. But her message was only too obvious. Gaffney sat down and began to write his confession. He told in great detail of Bessie's murder and of her visits from the grave. 'And now,' he said, 'there is no possible escape.'

Called by hotel staff, police broke into Gaffney's room the following day and found that the thief had hanged himself in a small closet. They read his confession and agreed at once that the case of the Soho strangler was now closed.

However, there was one element of the case which puzzled them. For the first time, a vital piece of evidence had vanished from the thief-proof vaults of Scotland Yard. It was a 'thuggee cord' – the cord with which George Gaffney had hanged himself.

The Isle of Dogs, that piece of land which juts out into the Thames and where the kings of England kept their hounds in olden days, lies in the infamous Limehouse area of London. It is an area which once formed the complex

Millwall and West India Docks and which has a long tradition of mayhem and murder.

In the early 1970s, a derelict warehouse at Radcliffe Wharf, on the Regent's Canal Dock, was being restored by a small group of contractors, who were said to have been disturbed on several occasions by the ghostly figure of a priest carrying a stick.

Many people claim that the sighting was purely imaginary and that the story of the ghostly priest was originated by a group of people wishing to prove how easy it was to create a ghost story and play on the imagination of the more credulous. Equally as many people claim that the sightings were real enough and that the hauntings refer to events which took place on the site in the 1860s, when the vicar of Radcliffe Cross set up a lodging-house for seamen in the area.

According to popular opinion, the vicar's main source of income was provided by murdering the seamen when they paid off after a long voyage, their remains being dumped into the convenient River Thames. The vicar's ghost, it is claimed, was regularly seen, usually in the evenings in the months of July and August and, according to one source, 'was the reason why the dock was always closed no later than five o'clock, as no one would work there after dusk'!

One of the more recent claims is of a sighting at 8.30 one Sunday morning in July 1971, when the head of the contracting firm claimed to have seen an elderly man with long white hair, dressed in black and carrying a cane, less than twenty yards away. So positive was the witness that this was a real person that he greeted the figure and began to walk towards him, thinking he might be ill. Suddenly the figure vanished. Other members of the team claim to have seen the same figure two hours later, and he was again seen the following Sunday at around ten o'clock in the morning.

A more tangible ghost haunted 'Second-Hand City' in West Kensington.

The Exhibition Hall at London's Olympia is linked with Fulham Broadway by North End Road, perhaps one of the busiest streets in West Kensington. Just along here once stood an old Methodist chapel.

The building had stood empty for some time, but in 1966 the *West London Mail* greeted the New Year with a story which not only embraced half a dozen facets of nastiness in one scoop but cleared the front pages for the horrifying court details of the murder of a sixty-five-year-old prostitute, whose naked and battered body had been found in the basement of the disused chapel a month earlier.

Annie Doonan was a well-known local character, and on the night of Saturday 4 December 1965 she had been drinking in a number of public houses in the area. She was last seen staggering drunkenly from the Old Oak Inn in North End Road at about 10.30 p.m. She was accompanied by a thirty-year-old man who lived at the nearby Salvation Army hostel. Both were obviously the worse for drink, but not so drunk that their intentions were not clear in both their minds.

Reaching the old chapel, both were seen to vanish into the basement, where two days later Annie's body was discovered. The man who had been seen going into the basement with her on the night she died was arrested almost immediately, making rather pathetic attempts to explain away his blood-stained clothing by saying that he had been in a fight with an unknown man in North End Road. Later, however, he made a statement in which he admitted that he and Annie Doonan had gone to the basement for the purpose of having sex and that in an angry quarrel which had broken out over the fee for her 'services' he had lost his temper and killed her. He was committed to the Old Bailey, where he was found guilty and given a life sentence.

The events of the night passed from the memory of those not personally involved and the old chapel found a new lease of life as 'Second Hand City', a market for bric-à-brac and old furniture.

Soon reports began to appear in the press which suggested that 'Second Hand City' was haunted. One man, who was in charge of the antiques section, told local reporters that he had seen 'a pinkish grey transparent shape with an indefinable outline, floating in the air'. He went on to say that there was a hint of a long robe and a hood, although it was not possible to distinguish a face.

An upholsterer, working late in the basement one night, claimed to have heard what he called 'unusual noises' coming from behind him and, on looking round, to have seen a phantom 'gliding round in a corner by some chairs that had just come in'. Despite his enthusiasm for the job, the upholsterer never worked late again after that. No one did. Then, one morning at about three o'clock a passer-by reported that all the lights were on in the old chapel, yet when the staff opened up the following morning, they said that the place was in total darkness.

If this was the ghost of Annie Doonan, it never gave off an air of remorse or regret. On the contrary, the atmosphere was one of happiness, delighting in Victorian surroundings. The figure would often be seen gliding down the stairs to the basement where there was a fireplace and two Victorian armchairs for the benefit of the staff during their tea-breaks and so forth. It was that area which was the favourite haunt of the spectre. Invariably it would disappear near the fireplace, but it could often by seen sitting by the fire, long after the armchairs had gone.

The ghost was seen several times over the years, nearly always around Victorian chairs, whenever they appeared in the store-room. Footsteps would be heard walking overhead when the building was known to be empty, and things would mysteriously disappear only to turn up again weeks or even months later. Was this the tormented ghost of poor old Annie, or was it linked with the earlier religious history of the building? No one knows.

Sitting quietly on a bench alongside a statue in Berkeley Square one warm Sunday morning and gazing at the ornamental railings behind which stand the premises of Maggs Bros, respectable antiquarian booksellers, I tried to imagine how it would all have looked more than a century ago. No nightingales sang then, only the cold north-east wind soughed down the chimneys of this old dark house, brooding and menacing; the paintwork peeling; the dead eyes of blank windows; a mass of brown and withered leaves; scraps of paper and the sprinkle of broken glass cluttering its neglected frontage.

No.50 Berkeley Square was famous as the most haunted house in London for well over a century, bringing Victorian visitors to the city, thronging to gaze and shudder at its grim and grimy façade, remote and sinister behind these same ornamental railings. Throughout Queen Victoria's reign, this forbidding house in the heart of Mayfair loomed prominently on the sightseer's list. Several hundred would make a special journey just to stand outside and stare at the capital's most ghostly building, reputed to be the scene of so many horrific happenings.

People were said to have been, quite literally, frightened to death in there. Others had been driven stark, raving mad by some appalling nameless horror that lurked in a haunted room on the upper floor. Over the years it has become more and more difficult to sift legend from reality, and tracking back on the trail of the horror house of Berkeley Square is not easy.

Once the home of Prime Minister George Canning, the house was built in the elegant eighteenth century, and it is possible that the ghost, or whatever, originates from that time. There are certainly enough stories – stories such as that of the little child, a pathetic wraith in a plaid dress, who was said to have been frightened to death in an upstairs nursery and who has been seen sobbing and wringing its hands in misery and anguish. Stories of a nameless man who went mad in an upper room, waiting for a message that was to be written by a ghostly hand on the wall of the room and which never came. *Other* messages appeared, so it is said, but never the right one for which he eagerly waited.

There is a story of a young woman who, rather than submit to the wicked wiles of her evil guardian, flung herself from the topmost window, and whose ghost could later be seen screaming and clinging to the window-ledge before hurtling to her death in the street below.

In 1830 pandemonium broke out in the house, even

though it was empty at the time. Night after night it was the centre of a great deal of weird poltergeist activity and, although it was unfurnished, there came from it the unmistakable sounds of massive furniture and heavy boxes being dragged across the bare floorboards. Bells were heard ringing all over the house, yet when investigators rushed in they saw nothing – except the bells still swinging eerily on their wire coils.

Occasionally a window in the empty house would be flung open and small objects, such as stones, old books and once a pair of spurs, would be thrown into the street by invisible hands. One morning, after a particularly noisy night, every window of the house that looked onto Berkeley Square had been smashed.

Many people put the blame for the disturbances on coiners, saying that it was they who made the weird sounds and showed ghostly lights in order to keep the inquisitive away while they carried out their nefarious activities at night in the empty house. However, the hard facts do tend to disprove this.

The first really 'hard' fact my research revealed is that in 1859 the Hon. Miss Elizabeth Curwen died there at the age of ninety. She had taken over the tenancy some years earlier from Lady Bromley. Sometime after Miss Curwen's death, a man called George Vincent testified that he had been in her service from 1851 until her death and that, although he had himself lived in at 50 Berkeley Square during that time, he had not found it to be haunted in any way. He added that it was not until 1864 that he had heard that the house had a reputation for being haunted.

In 1873 a report appeared in the *Weekly Times* that a Mr Myers of 50 Berkeley Square was being sued by the local council for taxes long overdue. A summons was taken out, and the newspaper stated that, 'The house in question is known as a haunted house by the neighbours.' It also added that it was believed that the neglect to pay the taxes arose because the occupier was an eccentric, an important point because it is held by many that it was the eccentricity of Mr Myers which gave rise to the ghost during his tenancy.

The story goes that Mr Myers was about to be married, and he took the house in Berkeley Square and set about furnishing it and making every preparation for what he believed would be his future happiness. Then his fiancée ran off with another lover. Myers was heart-broken, and the shock of the whole affair sent him mad. He became more and more of a recluse, eventually withdrawing into a small room at the top of the house, only opening the door to receive food from a manservant.

However, at night the recluse would issue forth from his tiny room. Gaunt and spectral-looking, he would flit through the once grand rooms below like some pallid ghost, the flame of his solitary candle flickering eerily over the mouldering, dust-sheeted furniture, bought so long ago to delight his unfaithful love. So, on the melancholy meanderings of poor Mr Myers, may have been founded the legend of the haunted house. He died in 1878, but it appears that his spectre was not interred with his bones.

In 1880 the house was taken over by a family called Bently, the family consisting of a father and two teenaged daughters. The elder girl was engaged to be married and it was agreed that her fiancé should come to stay at the house. Now up until this time none of the family had experienced anything of a supernatural flavour, although one of the girls had remarked on a strange, musty, zoo-like smell and thought she had heard an odd whimpering noise.

It was while the housemaid was preparing a room very late one night for the arrival of the elder girl's fiancé that a series of screams rang through the house, sending the whole family rushing upstairs.

Flinging open the door of the guest chamber, they were horrified to discover the housemaid lying on the floor at the foot of the bed. She was convulsing and her eyes were fixed with an expression of indescribable terror on one corner of the room. She was quickly taken to St George's Hospital, where she died the next morning, refusing to give any account of what she had seen.

Later that same day the fiancé – Captain Kenfield – arrived at 50 Berkeley Square. He was informed as to what had happened the previous night and was offered a different room. Firmly and politely, he insisted that he be allowed to occupy the room in which the tragedy had occurred. He did agree though, at the request of his fiancée, that he would sit up until past the fatal hour and that he would ring his bell if anything unusual happened.

The family waited in suspense. The clock on the staircase landing began to strike midnight, and the bell from the guest room rang faintly. As the clock chimes faded away, there followed a brief interlude of ominous silence – and then there was a tremendous peal of bells jangling throughout the house.

As one, the family rushed to the guest room. Captain Kenfield was frozen in the identical spot where the dead housemaid had been. As she had been, he too was convulsed and his eyes were rooted on the place where she had stared in terror. Captain Kenfield was never able to reveal the cause of his horror, and wisely the family soon left the house, never to return.

A somewhat nebulous story tells of a Mr Du Pré, who kept his lunatic brother locked up in one of the top floors at No.50. The poor man was so violent and deluded that no one dare enter the room and he was fed through a small hole in the wall. His bone-chilling moans and manic cries and howls were frequently heard by neighbours and passers-by in the street.

Today the reign of terror in Berkeley Square has ended. The house now stands in placid sunshine, the chaste premises of Maggs Bros. They report that since they took over the premises, just before the Second World War, not so much as a leaf has been wrongly turned. Is the horror ended or will the house one day awaken again from its slumber? We shall have to wait and see.

The exact number of children and young people who have been murdered will never really be known, for many murders have yet to be discovered and, of course, murderers have been known to escape justice, even though they were tried for their crime. Such a case was that of the murder of Jane Clouson of Kidbrook, London, in 1871.

Jane was a maidservant in the home of a Greenwich printer with the unlikely name of Ebenezer Pook. She was seventeen years old and a pretty young thing and was seduced by Pook's twenty-year-old son, Edmund. It was more than just an isolated seduction: the affair went on for some months, with the inevitable result that Jane became pregnant.

When Mr and Mrs Pook discovered what had been going on under their respectable, God-fearing roof, they dismissed Jane on the spot – although they later denied this as being the reason – and Jane, not unreasonably, turned to Edmund for support. Edmund, however, had no intention of supporting her and he certainly had no thoughts of marrying the girl. Jane was insistent that he should do the right thing by her in one way or another. She was desperate in a hard Victorian world, with no family or parents to turn to.

Edmund made her all kinds of promises which he had not the slightest intention of keeping, and he arranged to meet the girl at Blackheath on the evening of 26 April 1871. Early the next morning she was discovered battered and severely injured in Kilbrooke Lane. She died in Guy's Hospital a couple of days later without having regained consciousness. Edmund was arrested and stood trial for her murder, but the judge ruled that all the statements Jane had made in the weeks before her death which might incriminate him were hearsay and were therefore inadmissible as evidence. So Edmund Pook was found 'not guilty' and was subsequently discharged.

The verdict caused an uproar, and there were a number of disturbances in Greenwich. Apparently there was uproar in the next world too, for when Edmund had been released by the court, Jane's ghost returned to the scene of the crime and began to haunt Kilbrooke Lane. At the time, this was a part of London SW3, and it has been entirely re-built since the 1870s, the Kilbrooke Lane that Jane haunted having been completely built over.

The old Kilbrooke Lane was a popular resort for courting couples. It was narrow, shaded by trees and tall hedges and crossed by a small stream. The lane ran through cornfields and farmland and offered plenty of sheltered privacy for a spot of dalliance.

On the night of Jane's murder it had been patrolled at regular intervals by PC Gunn. The attack on her took place at about 8.30 and she was left lying by the side of the lane past which the police constable patrolled twice during the night without seeing her. Towards dawn she partially recovered consciousness and crawled into the centre of the lane, just as the constable came by a third time. Her face and head had been terribly battered with a lathing hammer which was later found nearby. (This was a long-handled tool with an axe opposite the hammerhead and made a very vicious weapon.) Lovers in the lane that night had heard her screams, but no one had troubled to investigate.

Over the years, Jane's troubled spectral screams were heard again and again by courting couples in Kilbrooke Lane, and her ghost was seen more than once by the patrolling policeman. She appeared in a long flowing white dress, her face running with blood. The cries continued to be heard until Kilbrooke Lane finally disappeared and the land between Eltham and Shooters Hill Road was gradually built on. Rochester Way now runs right across the old lane, completely obliterated with bricks and mortar. It was only when this happened that Jane's forlorn ghost deserted the spot where her wretched lover had battered her to death.

As a point of interest, Jane did have one champion on this earth, a man called Newton Crossland, who wrote a deliberate and libellous pamphlet after Edmund Pook was acquitted. He was taken to court for his troubles, but Pook received only nominal damages, thanks to Crossland's counsel, who put up a favourable case for justification, on the grounds that Pook *was* guilty of Jane's murder and would have hanged but for the judge's ruling about the hearsay evidence.

But a man cannot be tried twice for the same crime – at least, not in this world. Perhaps Pook's encounter with Jane in the next world afforded him his just deserts.

*

When the Coldstream Guards were stationed at Wellington Barracks in St James's Park in the 1870s, several sentries reported seeing the ghost of a headless woman walking from the old Cockpit Steps, in Birdcage Walk, towards the lake in the park.

In a sworn statement, one guardsman reported that at about 1.30 in the morning he had seen the figure of a woman rise up out of the ground no more than about two feet away from him. He was so terrified that he momentarily lost his power of speech as, eyes popping, for two or three minutes he watched the figure, dressed in a red-striped gown with red spots between each stripe, before it suddenly disappeared.

Another guardsman reported hearing shrieks and shouts coming from an empty building behind the Armoury House late at night. In his subsequent statement he said that the voices appeared to be shouting, 'Bring a light! Bring a light!', the voice dying away on the last word. Thinking that someone might have been taken ill, he tried to locate the origin of the cries and shouted back. Each time he did so, the voice answered him, repeating the same phrase, 'Bring a light! Bring a light!' Then he heard noises sounding as if the sash windows were being hastily lifted up and dropped, from different parts of the dark building.

The building was later searched. It had been empty for a number of years but, except for some deterioration, nothing was found which could account for the sounds of the opening and closing of the windows. The records were then searched for anything which might suggest a possible reason – whether rational or irrational – which might account for the increasing number of reports now reaching the commanding officer.

Going back over the history of the Foot Guards, it was discovered that in 1784 there had been some scandal attached to the Coldstreams, when a sergeant had murdered his wife and, in an attempt to make it difficult to identify the body, he hacked the head from her shoulders, before throwing the remainder of her corpse into the lake, from which it was later recovered.

His rather gruesome attempt to escape the consequences of the crime failed because five witnesses came
forward who were able to show that the gown – of cream
satin with red stripes and red spots between the stripes – in
which the body was clothed when dragged up from the
lake was the same one that the sergeant's wife had once
possessed.

Even today the headless spectre of the sergeant's wife is
still seen occasionally, roaming the historic streets and
passageways that surround St James's Park, sometimes
with blood spurting from the severed neck.

In 1975 a London taxi braked suddenly, the driver
staring with wide, unbelieving eyes at the macabre figure
that stepped in front of his vehicle. It looked like a woman,
although her red striped dress was so dated she could have
come from some West End Theatre production – except
that the form which glided smoothly but stiffly across the
front of his taxi did not have a head! Before the astounded
cabbie had time to think, the figure had vanished and the
street was empty.

All this took place early one bright spring morning in
Cockspur Street, early enough for no one to be around
and for the cabbie not to have picked up his first fare.
Unable to ask anyone if they too had seen the horrible
apparition, he sat quite still, his eyes fixed to the spot
where the headless figure had suddenly disappeared. It
was some time before he recovered enough to return to
the garage, where he related his unearthly encounter to
his mates. He was relieved to discover that he was not the
only person to have seen the headless ghost of the
sergeant's wife.

It was a bitterly cold winter evening. Dense fog blanketed
London, turning it into an unreal, two-dimensional city of
shadows. Nowhere was the fog thicker than on the
Thames Embankment, where it swirled round the grim
brick walls of New Scotland Yard.

Deep in the basement, the police officer in charge of the
notorious Black Museum sat working late amongst the
grisly collection of criminal relics of past murders and

violent death. Then, suddenly, the door to the museum opened and the officer was amazed to see a hooded female figure walk into the room. Thinking it was a nun, he walked forward to ask her what she wanted. As he did so, the figure suddenly vanished. Seconds later, it re-appeared at the far end of the room where, to his horror, the policeman saw that the hooded figure had no face!

In the broad light of the following day, the sceptics laughed at the story, saying that the hooded phantom was merely a drifting spiral of London fog, putting out clammy fingers to scare him. But the older police officers did not laugh so easily, for they remembered the Yard's very own gruesome murder mystery and the headless corpse which had been discovered on the very site of the Black Museum.

Before its removal to the present Broadway site, the world-famous New Scotland Yard, with its equally famous telephone number – Whitehall 1212 – stood near Westminster Bridge on land which had been reclaimed from the Thames, when the Victoria Embankment was built. Originally the site had been earmarked for the Grand National Opera House, but by the 1880s the scheme had run out of money and was abandoned, the building having proceeded no further than a vast underground labyrinth of brick passages and vaulted chambers. It was then that the Metropolitan Police took over the site to erect their new HQ on the foundations.

One morning in 1888 a carpenter was working on the construction of the new building in one of the dark underground vaults. He kept his tools in one particular vault, and when he went to get them, he saw an old coat bundled in a far corner, something he had not noticed before. He saw it again the following morning and, curious, went to examine it more closely. He discovered that it was actually a cloth-wrapped parcel, which he proceeded to untie. Suddenly he leapt back in alarm as the material fell away to reveal a headless, limbless human torso. He rushed to the nearby King Street police station and stammered out the story of his horrific discovery.

Post-mortem examination later revealed that the

remains were those of a plump, well-nourished woman, fair-skinned and dark-haired and aged about twenty-five years. Her head had been removed with a saw, as had the arms, pelvis and lower limbs, but they were able to calculate her height at about five feet eight inches. The doctors were unable to say how she had died, but the fact that the heart was pale and free from clots indicated that she had lost a lot of blood.

The police began intensive enquiries to try to discover the woman's identity, plugging quietly away at the case for several months, but they were never able to uncover the identity of the victim or her murderer. Eventually they had to admit defeat, and the file was closed, but Scotland Yard could never forget the gruesome murder right on its own doorstep.

It was inevitable that stories of an alleged ghost should begin to circulate, especially amongst the young coppers – but when the headless phantom actually appeared in the Black Museum, the older constables could not help wondering. Now the Yard has moved to new glass-and-concrete quarters, leaving many ghosts behind. But of all the strange mysteries that have passed through its old doors over the years, there was none that it would have liked to have solved more than the headless phantom in its own grisly basement.

2. Ghosts of Conscience

The great majority of hauntings, particularly those of the so-called 'Grey Ladies' who drift through many of our older houses, seem to be what can best be described as 'ghosts of conscience', often victims of injustice, appealing to the living for a decent burial or for their wishes to be respected, or just for sympathy. Some only seek peace, while others protest that their peace has been disturbed.

Raynham Hall, a magnificent stately home near Fakenham in Norfolk, has been haunted for 300 years by a woman dressed in brown and thought to be the ghost of Dorothy Walpole, sister of one of Britain's Prime Ministers, Sir Robert Walpole. Dorothy's father – also called Robert – was made guardian of a thirteen-year-old viscount, Charles Townshend, and as Dorothy and Charles grew up together, so they fell in love. However, when they wanted to marry, Dorothy's father refused his permission on the grounds that people would think the Walpoles were after the Townshend fortunes and vast estates.

Charles Townshend resigned himself to his fate and a short time afterwards married a baron's daughter. But Dorothy couldn't shake off her feelings towards him quite so easily, despite a wild whirl of parties. She went to London, then to Paris, and she soon scandalized the French social set of the day by setting up house with a well-known rakish aristocrat.

In 1711 Charles Townshend's wife died, and when Dorothy heard the news, she hurried home to Raynham Hall. Within a year, she and the widowed Charles were at last married. For a while they were blissfully happy, but then the inevitable happened: gossip about Dorothy's escapades in Paris reached her husband's ears. He was furious, confining her to her rooms and allowing her no visitors. Within ten days, Dorothy was dead. The records show that she died from smallpox, but local historians blame her death on a push from behind at the top of the hall's grand oak staircase.

It was not long before her ghost was seen by servants, family and guests alike.

In 1786 King George III was staying at the hall. Sometime during the small hours he suddenly woke up to see a brown-clad woman, her hair dishevelled and her face ashen, standing beside his bed. The King fled the bedroom in his nightgown and nightcap and stormed around the house rousing everyone, vowing not to stay another hour in the accursed place.

Alarmed at upsetting so royal a personage, the Townshends ordered a nightly watch by gamekeepers, and a few nights later they were rewarded with a sight of the woman in brown, walking down a corridor. One man stood his ground, challenging her – and she walked right through him. He said later that he had felt an ice-cold cloud pass into his bones and out again.

She appeared again in 1835. Colonel Loftus, brother of the then Lady Townshend, saw her on several consecutive nights leading up to Christmas, describing her as a stately woman in rich brown brocade with a cap-like head-dress. Her face was clearly defined, although where her eyes should have been there were only black hollows. The ghost appeared to several guests over the next few days, cutting short the Christmas merrymaking.

Two or three years later, the ghost of Lady Dorothy startled another distinguished guest, the author Captain Marryat, a tough sea-going man who had scoffed at the story of the hauntings. Invited to see the ghost for himself, Marryat stayed at the hall in a room where a portrait of the formidable woman was hanging. Late that same night, he and two other guests saw the ghostly figure walking the corridor near his room. They scuttled into a side room as the phantom approached, and watched as it stopped outside the open door, the eyeless face grinning wickedly at them. Captain Marryat was unnerved enough to grab his pistol and fire a shot which went straight through the still grinning figure and crashed into the door opposite.

The ghost was seen less frequently after that, but in 1936 she returned in a most dramatic manner. Two professional photographers, commissioned to take pictures of the hall for Lady Townshend, were setting up their camera to take shots of the oak staircase. Suddenly one saw a vapour form take shape, and he urged his colleague to expose the photographic plate. This he did, without knowing why. The flash caused the shape to vanish – but when the plate was developed, there on the stairs was the outline of a woman in a flowing veil and white bridal gown. Experts who examined the plate were convinced it was not a fake.

Had Dorothy decided to let the world know what she looked like on her fatal wedding day some 225 years earlier?

Spinster Hannah Beswick died over 200 years ago. Her body was embalmed, but her restless spirit still haunts Ferranti's factory, built on the land where her home once stood.

Hannah was a wealthy Lancashire landowner whose home, Birchen Bower, dominated several acres of fertile land at Hollinwood, on the outskirts of Manchester. She was a tough old girl, afraid of neither man nor beast, but when, in 1745, Bonnie Prince Charlie crossed the border into England and advanced south, she became so obsessed with the thought of the invading Scots that she hid all her money and valuables. They remained hidden for the rest of her life.

Scots apart, Miss Beswick's only other fear was of being buried alive – quite understandable in the light of what had happened in her own family. One of her brothers had fallen ill and, while unconscious, had been pronounced dead by the local doctor. Preparations were made for his funeral and he was laid in an open coffin so that relatives and friends could pay their last respects. While lying in his shroud, surrounded by flowers, he began to show signs of life and was hastily removed to his bed.

So when Hannah died in 1768 without divulging where she had hidden her fortune, because of what had happened to her brother, she took steps to ensure that her corpse was not buried. She left Birchen Bower to a young doctor, Charles White, on the condition that he have her embalmed and kept in a safe place above ground. For some reason, she also insisted that every twenty-one years her body should be taken back to Birchen Bower and allowed to lie in the granary for seven days and nights.

Hannah was duly mummified, her body coated with tar and wrapped in heavy linen bandages and, in accordance with her wishes, her face left uncovered. For many years Dr White faithfully kept her body at his own home, Sale Priory, but when he died it was moved to Manchester Natural History Society's museum, where it became a major attraction. A century after Hannah was embalmed, the commissioners of the Society, finding the museum overfilled with relics and needing room for new acquisitions, decided it was time she was given a proper Christian burial. She was finally interred at Harpurhey Cemetery on 22 July 1868, where her remains lie to this day.

But this was not the end of Miss Beswick. People began to claim to have seen her ghost drifting through the rooms of Birchen Bower, dressed in her usual black silk gown and white lace cap. After the burial of the mummified body, the ghost became more agitated, and she was often seen scurrying between the old barn and the pond as though deeply troubled. Sometimes the barn would glow as if it was on fire.

Birchen Bower remained empty for a number of years, inhabited only by the spectre of Miss Beswick. Then it was bought and converted into a number of small dwellings to be rented out to cotton workers and farm labourers. The new tenants were often to catch glimpses of her ghost, drifting, head bent as though deep in thought.

One aspect of her behaviour was puzzling. Often she

would disappear at a particular spot – a corner flagstone in the parlour in a part of Birchen Bower occupied by a handloom weaver by the name of Joe o'Tamers. Hannah's ghost seemed to hover about this room as if reluctant to leave it. One day Joe decided to pull up part of the flagstone floor to make a place to install a new handloom. To his amazement he found, hidden underneath the flagstones, a hoard of gold. He had discovered Hannah Beswick's fortune!

After this the ghost was seen with alarming regularity – no longer thoughtful but angry and menacing. People spoke of a brilliant blue light darting from her piercing eyes. At night she was seen near the pond, and sometimes weird noises were heard coming from the barn, but no one would dare venture inside to investigate after dark. All this gave rise to speculation that there were more valuables hidden nearby and that Hannah was determined to make sure that no one got their hands on them.

The hauntings continued until Birchen Bower was demolished. Ferranti's built a factory on the site, and that was thought to be the end of the affair. Then, a few years ago, a factory worker, an Asian immigrant who knew nothing of the story, ran screaming to his foreman one night, saying that he had seen the figure of a strange woman in an old-fashioned black silk gown and white lace cap.

The small village of Chipping, in Lancashire's beautiful Ribble Valley, is reputed to have more ghosts than inhabitants. The Sun Inn in the centre of the village is haunted by the ghost of a serving-wench who, in the mid-nineteenth century, committed suicide after being left at the altar.

Lizzie Dean was engaged to be married to a local farmer's son, but a few days before the wedding he told her that he loved someone else and that their engagement was off. Broken-hearted Lizzie took herself off to her room in the attic of the inn and hanged herself from a beam.

She left a suicide note in which she asked to be buried in

the pathway to St Bartholomew's Church, directly across the road from the Sun Inn, the reason being that, for the remainder of his life, her ex-lover would have to walk over her grave each week on his way to Sunday service and he would be forever reminded of the wrong he had done her.

Towards the end of the last century, extensive alterations were made to St Bartholomew's Church, and the path itself was re-sited. Lizzie's grave can still be found alongside the original path beneath an ancient yew tree – ironically directly opposite the window of her old room. These alterations to the pathway must have had an effect on Lizzie's restless spirit, for soon after her unhappy ghost returned to the inn where she had worked, where she had perhaps found much happiness and where she now made her presence known to landlord Ted Oakes on more than one occasion.

In a recent television interview, he told me that shortly after moving into the Sun Inn he became aware of odd happenings. As he was sweeping up the hallway one day after closing time, the telephone rang and, when he returned from answering it, the cigarette ends, crisp packets and other rubbish he had left in a pile in the centre of the hallway had disappeared. The broom he had been using was propped up against the opposite wall of the hallway from where he had left it.

He saw Lizzie's ghost on several occasions after that. One night, again after closing, when Ted was alone in the main bar, he watched a petite, cloudy figure wearing a long dress with leg-of-mutton sleeves, hair swept up on the top of her head, walk from the tap-room – which had originally been the kitchen, cross the hallway into the main bar and then walk through a piano and into the wall.

About a year later, it was decided to make a serving-hatch in the wall through which the figure disappeared, because it was thought that immediately behind it was the present-day kitchen and it would be quicker and easier to use the hatchway when serving hot bar-snacks at lunchtime. However, when work was begun, it was discovered that behind the wall was a door, over 200 years old, and some steps which led to a tiny drinking-room – a door through which Lizzie Dean would have passed frequently to and from the old kitchen in the course of her daily routine.

Margaret Leigh was born in Burslem, Staffordshire, about 1680. The exact date of her birth is not known, although we do know for certain when she died, for there was good reason to remember her death, and ensuing events struck terror into the hearts and minds of many.

In the seventeenth century Burslem was a small village surrounded by woodland, totally different from the centre of the pottery industry it is today, with rows of bland terraced houses standing where there once stood trees and where flowers and wildlife flourished.

Margaret was born into a well-respected and highly esteemed family. Her home was a comfortable Elizabethan farmhouse, and although the house was not very large, it was situated in extensive grounds. It seems that she was an ugly child and possibly malformed. Not a lot is known of her early childhood, but it is known that when she was older she moved away from her birthplace to live in a small, isolated cottage. Apparently her parents had turned her out of the family home for one reason or another, probably because life was becoming intolerable due to the fact that the local parson had proclaimed to all and sundry that she was a witch.

She managed to eke out a meagre living by keeping a few cows and selling milk, but even then whispers began to circulate that she not only gave short measure but watered the milk. Yet, despite all this, she appears to have been an enterprising young woman, for she later established a savings bank!

Living as she did in isolation, Margaret made friends with the birds and animals, in particular a blackbird which sat on her shoulder wherever she went. Perhaps it was because of this, coupled with the exaggerated squint which added to her ugly appearance, that people said she must be a witch and in league with the Devil – something which the local parson was quick to exploit.

The parson in question was a notoriously uncharitable

character, the Reverend Spencer, rector of the old church at Burslem, who appears to have taken more interest in his liquor than in his flock. This is borne out by his reputation for being able to drink any man under the table in the local inn, the Turk's Head. He crossed Margaret Leigh's path because she refused to attend church, and so, no doubt out of spite, he denounced her as a witch. At that time witchcraft was a crime punishable by death, yet not only does Margaret appear to have escaped conviction but there is no record of her having been a victim of any witch-hunt.

Margaret Leigh died in April 1748. The funeral took place on a cold and wet day, which Parson Spencer no doubt used as justification for a visit to the Turk's Head immediately after the interment. After several drinks in the inn, he suggested that he and some others should visit the dead woman's cottage and see if there was anything of value. On arrival, the parson walked boldly to the door, pushed it open and walked in, the others staying at a safe distance some way from the door. Suddenly from inside the cottage there was a loud howl, and Parson Spencer came rushing through the door as though the Devil himself was in pursuit. Speaking to no one, he fled past the others in the general direction of the Turk's Head, his face contorted with fear.

The other men, not knowing what had happened, followed after him, but it took several tankards of ale before he was calm enough to talk. He told his wide-eyed listeners that when he opened the cottage door he walked straight into the room and to his surprise found a fire burning in the fireplace, although no one had been inside the cottage for days. He then experienced a feeling of terror. His body went ice-cold and his eyes were drawn to one corner of the room, where, to his horror, he saw the woman he had buried less than two hours earlier sitting on her stool and looking at him with an evil smile on her face. It was a look of triumph!

From that time on, many people claimed to have seen her walking the streets of the village, and although few had liked her when she was alive, all were terrified of her when she was dead. People became so scared that no one dared go out at night, and they became even more terrified when the ghost of Margaret used to appear in the houses of village people and sit knitting in a corner of the room. They pleaded with Parson Spencer to do something to rid them of the terror.

An interesting account exists of the laying of her ghost which describes how Parson Spencer, along with five other clergymen, brought a stone pig-trough and, placing it in the centre of the church, prayed for hours that her spirit might find eternal rest. Eventually they saw her ghostly form hovering above them and, as they continued to pray, it slowly drew down towards them, face downwards. At last they got her into the trough and buried her in the churchyard.

Today the grave of Margaret Leigh can still be found in St John's Churchyard at Burslem – the headstone being the only one in a transverse position to the rest.

On the A1 about 1½ miles from Newport in Shropshire lies the village of Chetwynd. About two miles to the south-west of Chetwynd is the village of Edgmond. Both villages figure prominently in the story of hauntings by the ghost of Madam Piggott, hauntings which have gone on for well over 200 years.

She was the wife of the squire of Chetwynd Hall and was expecting her first baby. The squire hoped for a son who would inherit the estate, but there were complications before the birth, as Madam Piggott contracted smallpox. The doctor found himself in something of a dilemma and told Squire Piggott that he feared the loss of the unborn child or the mother. The squire callously replied, 'Lop the root to spare the branch!' His wife heard the death sentence pronounced by her husband, and one can only imagine the anguish she must have felt.

As fate would have it, neither mother nor child survived, and the distraught woman could find no rest for her soul, for within days her ghost was seen on a number of occasions emerging from a trapdoor on the roof of Chetwynd Vicarage, until it was demolished in 1864. Her ghost was also seen near a stump of an old oak tree in an area known as Windy Woods, the stump later to become known as 'Madam Piggott's Armchair'. There she sat weeping and combing the baby's hair.

At one time the apparition was quite troublesome in the area: many people saw her, and some were terrified. Fear became so intense that numerous clergy were called upon to exorcize the fearful earth-bound spirit – but without success. Modern roads carrying an ever-increasing amount of traffic have not in the least frightened the ghost away, for she walks the fields and lanes of the area to this day.

In the 1970s it was reported in the national press that a motorist had seen the figure in white cross in front of his car. Certain he had knocked someone down, the man got out, expecting to find a body, but to his amazement no one was there. The experience upset him considerably and he reported it to the police; they found nothing either. The driver had, without doubt, seen Madam Piggott, for by the roadside just where the incident took place is the graveyard in which her remains lie buried. One man had been riding past the area on his motorcycle when he was confronted by the ghost. When he accelerated to get away, he had the sensation of being followed.

About fifty years ago the ghost-hunter Elliott O'Donnell and two other men decided to investigate this apparition, which had caused terror among the local population by its awful appearance, for the ghost had the unpleasant habit of following them along the Windy Oaks, the lonely stretch of tree-sheltered road. It was not only the appearance of Madam Piggott which was frightening: there was also an accompanying unearthly noise which sounded like a deep-throated growl!

The ghost-hunting trio walked along the mile-long avenue of trees, the moon shining eerily through the twisted branches of the ancient gnarled oaks, the path almost ankle-deep in dead and rotting leaves, and the branches of the trees almost meeting over their heads. Not a sound broke the stillness of the night, save for the echo of their footsteps.

They reached a part of Windy Oaks from where Chetwynd church spire could be seen through the trees, and there they stopped and waited. Suddenly one of the men gripped O'Donnell's arm and pointed to a vibrating column of light among the trees. Then they all heard a long, low, unearthly, animal-like growl. The column of light, cylindrical in shape and about six foot in height, resembled a female form enveloped in a shroud. No limbs or features were visible, only a vague outline making erratic moves, first in one place and then in another. Again they heard the noise, this time sounding more like a snarl.

Not many yards away there was a small pool, and suddenly there was a tremendous noise seemingly coming from that direction. Wildfowl and moorhens screamed and birds in the trees began to make the most fantastic noises. The men had remained still and silent, so this wild disturbance could not have been caused by any movement of theirs. O'Donnell was later to recall: 'When we related our experiences at the local inn, no one laughed, as many of the people there had had similar experiences!'

The Senhouse family not only developed Maryport, in Cumbria, they also had a great share in the construction of one of the county's earliest railways, the Maryport & Carlisle Railway. Their family home was Netherhall Mansion, a pele-towered old house which, I believe, at one time housed a collection of Roman antiquities. It also housed a family ghost – a grey lady whose death occurred at the Hall in rather discreditable circumstances, probably at some time in the early nineteenth century.

The mansion, nearly 400 feet long and about sixty feet wide, mainly three storeys high, a maze of small rooms and passages, was a rambling conglomerate of architectural periods, beginning with its pele tower and some fourteenth- and fifteenth-century domestic rooms, with considerable extensions in the late eighteenth century and even more extensive work and additions towards the end of the nineteenth century; levels, passages, stairways and rooms were all something of a jumble. Throughout the last eighteen years of its life the Hall was unoccupied, its ground floor and some first-floor windows boarded up or massively shuttered from the inside. Neither gas nor electricity had ever been installed. Passages were uncommonly narrow, as well as dark, and movement had become extremely dangerous as the structure rapidly became derelict, with the assistance of substantial vandalism. Floors and ceilings rotted and fell, sometimes concealed by heavy plaster ceilings which crumbled and fell, covering up holes in the floor.

Up until the death of the Lord of the Manor in 1970, there had been relatively little structural deterioration, but thereafter it progressed with astonishing speed. The last Senhouse Lord of the Manor, a bachelor who inherited from his bachelor brother, had made his life in the south of England, and the mansion was left in the custody of a local resident.

He told me: 'I heard the characteristic movement associated with the Grey Lady on two occasions, when I was undoubtedly alone in the building, and I glimpsed her twice, once on the landing of the main staircase and once at a window on an attic floor.' However, it was during the last nine months of the Hall's existence that matters took a new turn.

'I was accustomed to finding the contents moved about or thrown around by the local vandals in rooms where there was natural light,' I was told, 'but the new development took the form of the movement of the massively heavy pieces of furniture – great cupboards, presses and wardrobes, for example – from one part of the Hall to another, and mainly in those parts which were in pitch darkness, and across obstructions from falling beams which had partially blocked the passages. I could not, and still cannot, reconcile this totally mindless activity and macabre results with local vandals, concerned only with loot.'

He went on to say that dimensionally he did not know how some pieces of furniture could have been moved as they were, even if doors and passages had not been obstructed with collapsed structure. 'The whole building seemed to have been taken over by some terrifying madness,' he concluded.

One evening, in 1973, the whole building was suddenly destroyed by fire. Though much of the timber was soaking wet, most of it covered by a thick layer of sodden plaster, the whole building was gutted, with considerable structural collapse in a blaze so fierce that medieval timbers over two feet square were burnt through. Although standing in its own grounds, Netherhall Mansion was less than five minutes drive from the fire station, yet the brigade had no chance. The fire authorities gave up all attempts at establishing the cause of the fire, but my confidant told me: 'With my intimate knowledge of the building and its condition immediately before the fire, I am equally at a loss and can see no other conclusion than to associate the strange occurrences of the previous few months with the Grey Lady as a fire-raising poltergeist.'

Today only the pele tower remains, although it too suffered serious damage, in addition to being gutted; it has now been restored as a shell. The internal masonry damage exposed a tiny closet, approached by a previously unknown tunnel about 2½ feet high, in the thick wall. This, it is believed, was in some way associated with the girl who was to become known as 'the Grey Lady'.

Round about the turn of the century, there stood a fine house in what was then the best residential area in Bristol St Michael's Hill. It was a house reputed to be haunted by what was described as 'a horrible, pale-faced servant girl'. The story goes that she was the natural daughter of the wealthy merchant who owned the house in the 1850s. She was said to have been a half-witted hunchback who always wore the same cheap pink dress and who lived a wretched, half-starved, often beaten life. In the end the poor girl drowned herself in an ornamental pool in the garden.

Early in the 1900s a widow and her daughters leased the house and very soon settled in quite comfortably, despite the fact that it seemed impossible to obtain the services of a housemaid. Yet soon after they had moved in, one of the daughters had passed a young girl busily sweeping the stairs with a hand-brush and dustpan as though her very life depended on it. The servant girl wore a cheap pink dress.

Thinking that her mother had obtained a temporary maid, the daughter gave the girl no more than a passing glance, yet at the same time she gained a distinctly unfavourable impression. The girl appeared to be untidy and sluttish, her cap soiled and askew; she was practically hunchbacked and she had such a white, unhealthy face.

The ghostly girl was next seen by another daughter, and this time she seemed aware of the daughter's presence, slithering down the stairs and grinning hideously over her shoulder as she slammed a door shut behind her. The same day a visitor to the house saw the repulsive spectre, describing her as a dishevelled maid in a dirty pink frock, who grinned wickedly before slipping away through a baize door leading to the kitchen.

Some weeks later, one of the daughters of the house, who was alone at the time, went down to the kitchen to get some hot water. Pushing open the kitchen door, she was again confronted by the sight of the dishevelled maid in the dirty pink dress busy at the kitchen range, her back to the door. Suddenly the figure swung round, an impudent leer on her deathly white face, and without a word of explanation she scuttled off into an adjoining pantry, from which there was no other exit.

Thinking that at last she was going to corner the girl and get some explanation from her, the daughter dashed into the pantry and was mystified to discover there was not a trace of her in there. Suddenly afraid, she turned and ran upstairs, only pausing for breath when she reached the landing. She practically died of fright when, looking up at the window, she saw the girl grinning at her from the outside – some thirty feet above the ground!

The daughter was later discovered in a dead faint in the porch and had to be sent away for several months until she had fully recovered from her shock. Needless to say, the widow and her other daughters moved out of the house as soon as possible, and as stories of the ghost spread, the house stood empty for many years – except perhaps, for the dishevelled maid in her dirty pink dress.

The old Victoria Military Hospital at Netley, near Hamble on Southampton Water, was built in 1856 and before its demolition in 1966 was long reputed to be haunted by the ghost of a nurse, thought to go back to the days of the Crimean War, who committed suicide by jumping from an upstairs window after discovering she had administered a fatal overdose to one of her patients.

There are several other versions of the origins of the ghost. One tells us that the spectre was that of a nursing sister who during World War I fell in love with a patient and, after finding him in the arms of another nurse, poisoned him before committing suicide. Another is that the patient died of his war injuries and the nurse jumped from the window because she was broken-hearted. Yet another claim is that this is the ghost of Florence Nightingale, who was mainly responsible for the building of the hospital, and that her frequent appearances around 1966 were an attempt to prevent its demolition. Whoever she was, her ghost was seen regularly over the years in one particular corridor.

Officials and staff at the hospital, a clergyman, visitors and patients have all told of seeing the figure, although stories of her appearance were often suppressed, because it was said that whenever she was seen a death would occur shortly afterwards. In 1936 a night porter reported seeing the spectral nurse pass a ward – and a patient died early the following morning. A night telephone-operator who had worked at the hospital for many years also claimed to have seen the ghost and heard the rustle of her dress as she passed. He said: 'There was a smell of delicate perfume in the air after she had disappeared!'

The ghostly nurse was said to have been particularly active when the building was being demolished, and the local press reported one witness as saying: 'The figure was dressed in an old-fashioned grey-blue nurse's uniform and was wearing a white cap. She was about twenty feet from me when I saw her and I watched her walk slowly away, making no sound, disappearing down a corridor which led to the chapel.'

Between 1969 and 1971, a strange female ghost appeared to at least three people in an old farmhouse which stands between Winchester and Bishops Waltham in Hampshire. This ancient farmhouse stands on a site where there is a continuous record of a dwelling as far back as Anglo-Saxon times.

In 1945 the old house was empty, standing nearly a mile from the nearest road, with no near neighbours, no water, sanitation or electricity, and it was beginning to decay after years of neglect, a sad sight under creeping ivy, overgrown brambles and elder. Then a couple saw it and recognized it as a place which could once more become a place of peace and beauty, and they bought it, restoring it to something like its former grandeur without destroying the main character of the house.

In 1970 the wife of the owner was sleeping alone in the farmhouse. Suddenly and for no apparent reason she found herself wide awake and, on opening her eyes, became aware of a figure standing at the foot of the bed. The figure was vague, looking rather like that of a slim woman wrapped in a cloak with a hood, yet the face stood out in natural colour and with great clarity. It was the face of a youngish woman, who appeared to radiate a great feeling of peace and tranquillity. She had lovely clear hazel eyes and a sweet, kindly expression. The woman and the apparition smiled at each other and, without any feeling of fear or nervousness, the woman turned over in bed and went back to sleep almost immediately.

About a year later, a man called at the farm on some sort of business and after a short while he asked, 'Is this house haunted?' Startled, the owner hesitated and the visitor said he had just seen a woman wearing a cloak and a hood. He said: 'She moved behind me and went out through that door!' Once again there was no feeling of fear or alarm; the visitor stressed that he felt only peace and tranquillity.

However, all this was to change a couple of years later,

when friends of the owners were invited to stay overnight – the friend's wife was a very beautiful woman, I am told. After an evening of general conversation over drinks, following dinner, the guests retired to bed. In the small hours of the morning, the wife woke up very distressed and calling out, 'She wants my body! She's trying to get inside my body!' Her husband soothed her, saying that she had been having a bad dream, and after some time the woman composed herself and eventually went back to sleep.

It was not until many months later that the husband returned alone to the farm, and only then did he tell the owner and his wife of the terrifying nightmare his wife had experienced when they both stayed there. He was totally unaware of the previous sightings of the hooded woman, and went on to say that his wife had told him of the ghost in her dream who had desired to possess her body. She said she had been a beautiful woman, possibly in her thirties, with hazel eyes, and she had a worn a cloak with a hood.

I'm told that since that time many others have stayed at the farm, but the beautiful apparition has not, so far as I am aware, been seen, which makes this haunting all the more puzzling and poses many questions. Perhaps among those who lived and died here over the centuries there is one who was repressed, guilty, jealous or indeed very happy – who for some reason is unable to rest. But why should she appear in this strange and unpredictable form?

The wedding dress on the skeleton crumbled to dust at the touch. The plain gold ring on the third finger of her bony hand had long since lost its lustre, and beneath the other hand, still held in the bony fingers, was a sprig of mistletoe that the young bride had carried with her on that fateful day so long ago. But the mistletoe was as withered and decayed as she was, a once lovely teenaged bride in her oaken coffin.

The oak chest's grim contents solved a still-remembered mystery of a tragic wedding day and a disappearing bride. Her name was not known, so she became known as 'the

Mistletoe Bough Bride', whose sad-eyed ghost still haunts Bramshill House, former home of the Cope family and now a police training establishment at Hartley Wintney in Hampshire.

Legend tells us that the young bride was married on Christmas Day in about 1725. Young and in a merry mood, she suggested a game of hide-and-seek and dashed from the room with a sprig of mistletoe in her hand. In a remote corridor of the old building she hid inside an exquisitely carved oak chest, still to be seen at Bramshill House. Once inside, the spring lock snapped shut, imprisoning her, despite her frenzied cries and hammering. Here she remained, unknown to her frantic husband, her father and the wedding guests, who searched in vain for hours – then days – for the missing girl. She was not found for over fifty years.

Over the past forty years there have been a number of sightings of the sad spectre in a white dress in the vicinity of the old oak chest. Shortly after the Second World War, King Michael and Queen Maria of Romania and their children lived for a time at Bramshill, and they claimed to have seen the ghost at various times. At first the children spoke of 'a lady in white' who passed through their bedroom without opening the door. Then Queen Maria saw her for herself, a beautiful young woman with a sad face, sitting in a chair, when the Queen thought she was alone in a room. When Maria spoke to her, the figure vanished.

A footman once reported that he awoke late one night to find the 'white lady' standing by his bed. He quickly jumped out and tried to embrace her, and as he did so, she simply dissolved in his arms, leaving behind a strong smell of flowers.

This smell of flowers is constantly referred to in reports of the ghost, being described as like the perfume of lily-of-the-valley. Some people, not knowing of the ghost, have walked into the house in midwinter and remarked with some surprise that they could detect the scent of lilies-of-the-valley hanging in the air. There have also been numerous reports of inexplicable and sudden drops in temperature, particularly in the area around the bridal chest.

Quite recently a senior police officer saw the ghost, and he admitted standing 'chilled with fright', the hair on the back of his neck bristling. He said that the phantom stood looking at him for a few seconds before evaporating into a mist and disappearing.

Late one night in 1985, one of the Bramshill security men was on duty alone in the house and in sight of the chest, when the sudden whiff of flowers made him look up. The beautiful, sad ghost was standing no more than ten yards away from him, by the chest. He later reported that, although she did not appear to be solid, he could not actually see through her either. The man described her as 'a young woman, dressed in a long white gown, and surrounded by an air of great sadness'. He said he did not feel afraid of her and they looked at one another for well over a minute, until a colleague came into the hall and the figure faded and disappeared.

It seems that after nearly three centuries, the sad phantom still seeks her bridegroom, who, long ago, went sorrowfully to his own grave.

Seeing a ghost can often be a harrowing experience, but what can be more harrowing and gruesome than seeing a ghost without a head? A particularly sinister example of this is the headless woman who haunts Kilworth House on the edge of Dartmoor in Devon. She is said to walk the landings and staircase of this gloomy old mansion which sits baleful and brooding on the desolate landscape.

Her footsteps are so real that many people swear to have actually heard the floorboards creak as she passes. Although she is headless, the empty space where her face should be is framed by a gauze-like head-dress, which sweeps in long folds down across her shoulders.

No one is really sure who she is, but tradition says she is the ghost of the daughter of Judge Glanville, a ruthless man who never allowed compassion to stand in the way of his duty. He is said to have sentenced his daughter to death during the reign of Queen Elizabeth I, her head being hacked from her shoulders by a series of blows by the bumbling executioner. The reason for her execution is said to be that the judge's daughter and her lover were accused of murdering a man whom her father had wanted her to marry.

Over the past dozen or so years, at least seven people have claimed to have seen the ghost of the headless girl. After the initial shock and revulsion at the horrible sight, they see her as a pathetic young thing, bent with grief, with a sparkling shimmer where her head should be.

Perhaps one of the most terrifying headless figures was seen during the winter of 1937, when a lorry-driver, snowbound with his lorry on the bleak Stainmoor Pass in Cumbria, was forced to sit in his cab all night until assistance came to help dig him out and get him on his way again. To keep himself warm, he climbed down from his cab and took a walk in the cold early morning air. Suddenly, to his absolute horror, he saw a headless woman riding on a large horse at an amazing speed across the moor. In doing so, he confirmed a legend which has been prevalent in that area for many centuries.

Some 900 years ago, a Saxon chieftain lived in a rude fortress on the edge of Stainmoor, who acknowledged no king as his master. Between himself and a Norman called Fitz-Bernard, whose stronghold was nearby, there was a bitter hatred over the right to chase over the moor, which both men claimed as their own. On more than one occasion the two men had come to blows, and in one encounter several retainers and the young daughter of Fitz-Bernard were taken prisoner. The Saxon chieftain wanted to make the girl his wife. He was well smitten by her beauty and fell madly in love with her, affording her all the kindness and courtesy possible while she was his prisoner.

All his attempts to woo her came to nothing and, after remaining a prisoner for some time, she was finally rescued by the Normans. As she was being borne in triumph across the moor, the Saxon chieftain appeared on the scene with a large number of retainers and charged wildly into the group of would-be rescuers who, outnumbered, were unable to withstand the onslaught. The Saxon, furious at the thought of losing his fair captive, severed her head from her body with one savage stroke of his sword.

Ever since that day, the headless horsewoman has been sighted quite frequently, galloping silently across the moor near Stainmoor Pass – the last recorded time by the lorry-driver, fifty years ago.

Finally a tragic headless ghost which can be found in a girls' school in the Crossgates area of Leeds, in Yorkshire. In the 1830s this rambling old building was an orphanage run by an order of nuns.

One day, two small children were locked in a room at the top of the building as punishment for some minor offence, when fire broke out on the floor beneath them, leaving the two children trapped. Hearing their screams, the young nun who had punished them raced upstairs in a rescue attempt. Fighting her way through smoke and flames, she managed to reach the room. She forced open the door and dragged the two children clear of the flames which had by now surrounded them. Just as she pushed the children to safety, a heavy beam fell and struck the heroic nun with such force that she was decapitated.

In recent years, the room where the nun died was the school sick-bay, but it had to be sealed off after several girls reported seeing the headless figure of the nun walk through the wall, and when others complained of hearing shrieks and of the appearance of flames licking the walls.

3. Old Soldiers Never Die

Early in the 1950s, a young apprentice plumber was working in the cellars of the Treasurer's House directly opposite the Minster at York. He was standing on a step-ladder when he suddenly heard the curious note of a trumpet blast drifting through the thick cellar walls, a noise that grew louder and louder.

Then slowly through the solid cellar wall emerged a horse and rider. The horse was big, shaggy and muscular, and on its back rode a man wearing the uniform of a Roman soldier. The surprise proved too much for the startled apprentice, who fell off his ladder with shock, continuing to stare dumbfounded as more and more figures emerged from the wall, this time on foot. The foot soldiers wore rough sandals and green tunics and stumbled dejectedly behind the horseman. The apprentice got to his feet and fled in terror, thus probably becoming the last citizen of Eboracum to flee from the Romans.

Several similar and equally reliable sightings of the Roman ghosts have been reported since, and it is now known that the Treasurer's House was built on top of a major Roman road.

A strange story exists concerning the Roman fort at Bowes, near Barnard Castle. The legion's recall to Rome and the locals' knowledge of the soldiers' disregard for discipline led to their wholesale pillage of the fort: before the garrison was deserted, the peasants invaded it and slaughtered every soldier in sight. Everything of value had been carefully buried by the Romans, who had evidently every intention of returning to Bowes, so the locals, though they searched high and low, found nothing and were cheated of the gold and valuables they had intended to steal.

For centuries the place has been shunned after dark, and particularly on the anniversary of the massacre, for each year on that date the ghosts of the slain Roman soldiers are said to appear, busily engaged in burying the gold. An old wives' tale? Well, it is recorded that some years ago two local men hid within the ruins of the fort on the anniversary night. Afterwards, in a sworn statement, they claimed to have seen a procession of phantom Roman soldiers bearing a huge chest of gold, which they then proceeded to bury.

The treasure remains hidden to this day, but both men who swore to seeing the Roman soldiery died violent deaths a short time afterwards!

The George and Dragon Inn, situated in Liverpool Road in Chester, is a quite modern public house built on the site of a 1,600-year-old Roman cemetery. This building is reported to be haunted by the measured tread of a Roman soldier on eternal sentry duty. Unexplained and unmistakable footsteps are regularly heard pacing the upper floor of the inn, from one end to the other, in the early hours of the morning. Twenty minutes later they are heard coming back – and apparently passing through solid brick walls in the process!

Maryport, in Cumbria, was developed as a coal port in the eighteenth century and was named after the wife of Humphrey Senhouse, the developer of the port. The Romans knew it as Uxelodunum and they defended it with a fort, Aluana, situated on elevated ground with a double ditch and wall for protection. To the south of the fort was a levelled parade ground and immediately adjacent to this the Tribunal. Also attached to the fort and post was an extensive civil settlement which spread over seventy acres along the headland.

One bright summer morning in 1954, a very young boy rushed home from the path – which ran between his home and the site of the fort – where he had been walking with his nanny, a lady who had been with the family for a number of years. The nanny said that she had to get him home as he had been terrified by what he described as a cart, drawn by two horses, which had come down the path towards him. He was trapped between the high stone walls on either side. He told his parents that the cart filled the path and he could not get out of the way. It was travelling fast. He said that it had two wheels and that a 'man in a shiny hat was driving it'. Nanny saw nothing of this and had no idea what had caused his sudden hysterical panic. From his description, his parents learned that the horses were harnessed to either side of the shaft – they were not in tandem.

Dimensionally it was impossible for a pair of horses to drive along the pathway, let alone at speed. But perhaps the walls were real only to the small boy, for he was too young to know about a *biga*, the two-horsed chariot used by the ancient Romans, in which the horses were harnessed abreast and not in tandem.

Recently the author learned that over the past couple of decades, on at least two widely separate and well-documented occasions, the level parade ground of the old fort of Aluana – now no more than a field – has been seen to be full of moving figures. Both occasions have been late at night in good moonlight, and on both occasions there was no stock in the field and the night was calm and cold.

Chingle Hall at Goosnargh, near Preston in Lancashire, is credited as being the most haunted house in England, and amongst its many recorded spectres is that of a Roman soldier.

In the 1920s Chingle Hall was occupied by the Longton family, no strangers to tragedy. Their only son hanged himself in the barn nearby and their daughter, at the tender age of sixteen, was going upstairs one day when she suffered a stroke from which she was not to recover. One day, just before she died, she claimed to have seen a Roman soldier walking down the stairs.

For years this story was taken with a pinch of salt,

considered by many to have been the delirious ramblings of a dying girl – until recent years, when someone took a photograph in the Great Hall of what was described as a cold spot. When the photograph was developed, it showed that the photographer had included the mirror which was on the wall in one corner of the room – and reflected in the mirror was the image of a Roman soldier.

The ghosts of Roman soldiers have long been said to haunt Mersea Island in Essex. Some accounts tell of a lonely Roman soldier being joined by other legionaries, following which the clash of swords is heard across the Saltings. Another account tells of an elderly woman who thought she once walked with a ghostly Roman soldier from East Mersea Road to the Causeway, describing the steady tramp of his feet beside her.

In early 1970 two naval ratings were driving over The Strood when something 'loomed up in front of the car; something dark, upright, with vertical and horizontal white lines on it, like the metal skirt of a Roman tunic'. It was a very clear night, yet they were onto the figure before they realized – and then they were through it! There was no bump, and although 'it' seemed to have no definite shape, they said, 'It resembled a human figure which was surrounded by mist.'

Lympne Castle near Hythe, in Kent, is described as being 'a romantic medieval castle with an earlier Roman, Saxon and Norman history'. It was also once the home of Thomas à Becket before he became Archbishop of Canterbury.

Rebuilt around 1360 on the foundations of what was thought to be a Roman watchtower, Lympne Castle is haunted by the ghost of a Roman sentry who, while on watch, accidentally fell to his death. His ghost is still said to be heard from time to time, treading the stone steps of the east tower. The 'click' of the gate below the castle walls heralds his coming, then the sound of his footsteps mounting the tower steps. After a few minutes silence, he is heard inside the building, but he is never heard coming back down again.

According to the Church and government teachings of bygone days, the greatest crimes against nature were killing a king and waging civil war. Both happened in Britain over 300 years ago, when Oliver Cromwell's Roundheads defeated the Royalist Cavalier armies and beheaded King Charles I. Ghostly echoes of that catastrophic conflict have lingered around the country ever since.

Edge Hill, on the borders of Warwickshire and Northamptonshire, was the scene of one of the bloodiest battles of the Civil War, on 12 October 1642. At the end of the day, the fields were littered with the dead and dying, and both sides withdrew to continue the war elsewhere. The following Christmas Eve, a group of shepherds were hurrying home at around midnight when they passed the battlefield. The sound of approaching drums, the clatter of arms, and the awful groans and screams of dying men stopped them in their tracks.

Before they could take to their heels, the rival armies materialized all around them, eerily lit colours blowing in the wind as they blazed away at each other with musket and cannon. This bizarre spectacle continued for more than three hours, finally fading at just after three o'clock on Christmas morning.

Over the years, the sounds and sights of war have been reported many times by people passing Edge Hill, although the fighting has never been as vivid as that on the first Christmas, something which Charles I declared was 'a sign of God's wrath against those who wage civil war'.

Three years after Edge Hill, Cromwell's forces routed a Royalist army at Naseby in Northamptonshire, and for nearly a hundred years generations of villagers from miles around gathered at the site on the anniversary of the battle to watch it re-enacted in the skies and listen to the din of the guns and the groans of the victims.

A phantom army which appeared – or seemed to appear – at Souter Fell in Cumbria had no connection with an actual battle but, as at Edge Hill, it appeared several times and was seen by a host of witnesses, creating something of a sensation at the time, and no wonder, for the marching columns of armed men, seeming to appear from nowhere, continued to pass across the eastern face of the mountain for an entire hour.

This weird spectacle was first witnessed on Midsummer's Eve in 1735, by a farmhand at Blakehills, about half a mile from the base of the mountain. Looking up, he was surprised to see the eastern side of its summit covered with marching troops. They came in distinct bodies from an elevation on the north end and disappeared into a cleft in the summit.

The farmhand's story was both disbelieved and ridiculed by everyone – they said he must have been drinking too freely. However, two years later his employer, farmer William Lancaster, saw the same phantoms, again on Midsummer's Eve. In glancing up at Souter Fell, he saw a few men following their horses on the mountain and at first took them to be returning hunters. When, about ten minutes later, he looked up again, he was astonished to see that the same figures were now mounted and were being followed by a great army of troops, marching five abreast in distinct bodies, each under the control of a mounted officer who rode to and fro along the ranks. As evening approached, discipline seemed to relax and various sections of troops intermingled, moving at unequal speeds, until the darkness swallowed them up. All the Lancaster family had seen the phantom army, but their story was no more believed than was that of the farmhand two years earlier.

However, on 23 June 1745, ten years after the original sighting, the Lancaster family gathered together twenty-six people to keep watch on Souter Fell with them. All were to witness the same spectacle as before – and more besides, for this time carriages were interspersed with the troops, a 'multitude beyond imagination', who filled the space of half a mile. They marched quickly until darkness fell and hid them, still marching.

Over the years the phantom army has been seen occasionally on Souter Fell, the last time in the 1930s, but like that at Edge Hill and Marston Moor it has never been explained. Was the entire cavalcade a procession of ghosts re-enacting some military operation of times long forgotten, or was it a trick of nature? Perhaps the past is always with us, perpetuating history like some lively book of record.

Mr and Mrs Reeves, who lived in the village of Holme Hale in Norfolk, had been visiting friends one evening, returning home at some time after two in the morning. There was a full moon and a few patches of mist when Mrs Reeves got out of the car to open the garage door for her husband. Suddenly she heard shouting in the near distance and she drew her husband's attention to it, thinking that someone was in trouble and in need of help. Her husband could not hear anything.

Within a few seconds the shouting was taken up by other voices, and now Mr Reeves could hear it also. The clamour was accompanied by the sound of many running feet, and he remarked that it seemed to be coming from a point a few hundred yards away from the far side of the bridge. Disturbed but curious, the couple moved into the roadway for a better view, but nothing could be seen. The noises continued, now augmented by the rattle of accoutrements and the hoof-beats of galloping horses.

At the time, thoughts of the paranormal did not cross their minds. Mr Reeves assumed that the horses they could hear belonged to a neighbouring farmer, and he was more concerned with stopping their flight. The shouting and the galloping drew nearer – but the village street remained empty of anything visible. The sounds were now so loud that whatever was causing them appeared to be milling round the couple and around the forecourt of the Red Lion Inn opposite. There was also an added sound, that of sticks hitting swords.

By this time Mr and Mrs Reeves were bewildered and a little afraid. They shrank against the wall of their house in an attempt to get away from whatever was causing the crashing sounds around them. Eventually the noise shifted away from them and appeared to move into a field across the road, next to the inn, before finally moving up the hill away beyond them and fading into the distance. After that, all the dogs in the village began to howl and carried on howling for several minutes.

Later BBC Television sent a crew to investigate the incident for their 'Timeslip' series. Their own researchers revealed that, although there had never been a pitched battle in the neighbourhood, as at Edge Hill or Marston Moor, there were a number of incidents recorded in Norfolk history which could have caused the disturbances experienced by Mr and Mrs Reeves. The most likely was thought to have been a series of serious riots during Ket's Rebellion in 1549, in which some of the rebels fled from Castle Rising to Watton, their line of retreat taking them directly through Holme Hale. It is on record that they had a camp a short distance away, at Hingham, which was attacked by troops under the command of Sir Edmund Knyvett – and the battle was fought between peasants and soldiers, the peasants using staves, the soldiers using swords.

One of the best-known ghostly warriors gained considerable publicity in the years leading to the Second World War. Lawrence of Arabia was a legend during his own lifetime, and the rumours which spread following his death in a motor-cycling accident in 1935 were no less legendary. At first they concerned aural phenomena, such as the roar of the Brough Superior which he loved to ride in the vicinity of his home, Clouds Hill, in Dorset.

The house stands about 1½ miles from the junction of the A35 Dorchester road and the B3390 at a place called Woodock crossroads. It is now National Trust property and is open to the public. People working and living nearby have claimed that Lawrence's motor cycle could be heard roaring towards them, usually around dawn. The noise would end suddenly when still some distance from the listener. With some justification, they claimed that there was no chance of mistaking the unique throaty roar of a Brough Superior's engine once it had been heard, and when Lawrence lived at Clouds Hill, it was heard quite often.

The naturalness of the sound of the motor cycle heard after Lawrence was dead helped give rise to some of the rumours which spread from Dorset to the rest of Britain around 1939 – rumours that the accident had been faked in order to allow Lawrence to be spirited away to the Middle East, where he was gathering support from the Arabs against Nazi Germany. Others went so far as to suggest that there was a plan to erect a statue of Lawrence of Arabia on a vacant plinth in Trafalgar Square, but this had been rejected by Prime Minister Chamberlain and his government, because the statue could not be erected while the subject of the sculpture was still alive!

The sound of the motor cycle was not the only clue to the continued existence of Lawrence on this earth – mortal or otherwise. Stories began to circulate of a figure dressed in Arab robes seen going into Clouds Hill at night. Lawrence, it was said, would appear in public whenever England was in danger, a modern parallel to the belief in Drake's drum.

Sir Francis Drake is without doubt one of the most famous ghosts in Devon, and he has reputedly haunted the Plymouth area for the last 400 years or so. Legend tells us that, if his drum is beaten, his spirit will be summoned and will emerge from Buckland Abbey and place his sword at the disposal of the monarch.

During the blitz on Plymouth during the Second World War, local people, sleeping in the countryside while the raids were in progress, told of distinctly hearing the drumbeats to the north of them above the racket of anti-aircraft fire and exploding bombs. (It is interesting to note that Drake's former home, Buckland Abbey, stands about eleven miles to the north of Plymouth.) Some people believed this was a supernatural sound, others that it was the authorities themselves summoning Drake to help them! Whatever the reason, the sound has never been explained away satisfactorily.

Other tales tell of Drake's phantom riding pell-mell from Tavistock to Plymouth in a black coach, the lurching vehicle pulled by headless black horses. Headless hounds run in front of the coach, and screaming devils fly about at the rear!

A man in armour, seen in the vicinity of the A2 road between Bexley and Dartford in Kent, is thought to be the ghost of the Black Prince. This figure is completely black, his features not seen due to the fact that the vizor of his helmet is closed. As in the case of Lawrence of Arabia and Sir Francis Drake, after the death of the Black Prince in 1376, rumours were widespread throughout the Home Counties that his ghost would re-appear – as indeed it did during the unsettled reign of his son, King Richard II – and that he would rise to do battle with any real danger to England.

This story has persisted for centuries, and periodically the ghost has been reported in times of great crisis, the last time being in the autumn of 1940, when the invasion scare was at its height. Among the many messages about spies asking the way, flashing lights signalling enemy planes and German parachutists dropping from the Kent skies, the police had reports of a man in armour striding out down the Dover road. These accounts were factual and free from any hysteria, and the official view was that this was the work of a practical joker, risking his neck by wandering around in the black-out amidst bombs and anti-aircraft shells. However, the unofficial view was that this was no joker. This was indeed the Black Prince, come to help England in her finest hour!

Bircham Newton Airfield, near King's Lynn in Norfolk, created quite a lot of interest in 1972.

This desolate airfield on the northern coast of Norfolk was constructed in 1914 and left derelict between the wars, only to be re-commissioned in 1939 at the onset of the Second World War, when RAF, Royal Australian Air Force and Royal Canadian Airforce personnel were stationed there.

Some years after the war, the old officers' mess was converted into a hotel for use by executives and guests of a construction training company which had taken over the site. Another part of the building was leased to an industrial film unit, for use as a studio whilst they made management training films. Some distance away, behind the hotel, is a single building converted into a squash court with two playing areas, and it is one of these courts which is haunted.

The first indication that something wasn't quite as it should be occurred one evening, when a player glanced up at the gallery overlooking the courts and saw a man in RAF uniform gazing down. Puzzled, he stopped his partner, and they both watched as the airman walked along the gallery to the doorway at the end and disappeared.

Because of their conviction that they had seen a ghost, the two men arranged for a tape-recorder to be left in the affected squash court overnight. It seems they had intended to stay with the machine but were too scared at hearing loud footsteps walking along the gallery. (It should be pointed out here that only one key existed for the building, which the two men ensured was locked once they had set the tape-recorder going.)

They returned later, once the tape had run out, and what they heard when it was re-played was extraordinary. They heard the sound of an aircraft, voices and clanking machinery – uncannily like the noises of a busy aircraft hangar in wartime. But even more disturbing were the strange, unearthly groaning noises. Thousands of radio listeners have since heard the tape-recording, which was analysed by a BBC engineer, who admitted he was mystified. There was no fault with the recorder; few noises could have penetrated the nine-inch brick wall; the tape was brand new, so old recordings could not have come through. One highlight of the recording was the sound of a woman's voice saying two words, but because of the background noises – a metal bucket being placed on the floor, a loud saw-like buzzing sound and a peculiar 'pinging' sound – the words were indistinguishable. Another puzzling aspect was the drone of the aircraft, which could be clearly heard, although checks revealed that no aircraft had been flying in the vicinity on the night the recording was made.

Determined to discover more about the ghost, a medium was called in and a seance arranged. The medium, on entering the squash court, went into a trance and began to sob, talking of a plane – an Anson – which caught fire and crashed behind a local church, killing three airmen, Dusty Miller, Pat Sullivan and Gerry Arnold. When he came out of the trance, the medium was able to explain that the three airmen had been keen squash players, and they had made a pact that, if ever anything was to happen to them, they would try to meet up again in the building. The medium concluded that after the crash the airmen had been earthbound at the airfield, because they had no idea the crash had killed them!

During the height of the investigations, the BBC *Nationwide* television programme sent along an intrepid female reporter to spend the night locked inside the haunted court with a tape-recorder. She later described the intense feeling of cold, the sounds of doors banging open and shut, and the peculiar fact that at exactly 12.30 the tape-recorder suddenly stopped for no reason at all.

Later enquiries revealed that the airfield had been haunted for years. A student attending one of the construction courses had his bedclothes pulled off him in the middle of the night by an invisible assailant, and another had his curtains torn and thrown across the room. A senior engineer claimed that he had been tapped on the shoulder a couple of times, whilst working alone in the attic of the officers' mess. He was so scared that he refused to work there again. One man claimed he had seen a figure in an RAF uniform walk through a solid brick wall in the old billiards room, which had been built since the war. He was so afraid that he refused to complete the course, and he left the following day.

Checks of wartime records reveal that a plane did indeed crash behind Bircham church, killing the crew of three. The hotel was finally demolished late in 1972, leaving the mystery of the haunted squash court still partly unanswered.

A young collector of military souvenirs knew whom to blame when he returned home to discover his tailor's dummy, resplendent in SS uniform, hurled from its regular place in the hall of his home. Only days before, the young man and his wife had been given the shock of their lives when an RAF pilot, complete with World War II flying-jacket, helmet and oxygen mask, appeared in their Croydon home. Clearly the patriotic spectre didn't appreciate finding a reminder of his old enemy in his new haunt. These events took place in 1978.

The young couple, who wish to remain anonymous, called in the Society for Psychic Research and told an investigator that the RAF pilot had appeared four times: first in his wife's bedroom as she changed to go out to dinner, then in the lounge, where the husband was relaxing watching television, and twice more in the bedroom, once when the wife was ironing and once when they were both together.

After that they saw him no more, but his invisible spirit began to play tricks on them and their guests. First he hurled the offending tailor's dummy about ten feet across the hall. Then he turned up in the spare bedroom, where a young married couple were staying as guests. In the middle of the night, the man got up to go to the bathroom and, while he was away, his wife felt the saucy spectre wrench the bedclothes from her naked body!

This was the last straw so far as their hosts were concerned, and they called in a local clergyman to exorcize the unruly spirit. But even during the exorcism ceremony the cheeky young pilot could not resist one final prank. The wife felt her bra-strap being plucked, although no one was standing anywhere near her at the time!

Research has revealed that the couple's home was on an estate built on the site of the old Croydon airfield, but who the saucy pilot was, or why he suddenly decided to make himself at home with the young couple, is anybody's guess.

Croydon was one of the first purpose-built airfields to be constructed in Britain. As far back as 1915, land around the airfield was used as an air defence base for London during the Zeppelin raids. By 1920, the old World War I airfields had developed into Croydon Aerodrome, and between 1920 and 1930 massive investment and development

turned Croydon into what was then the most modern
aerodrome in the world. Amy Johnson flew from there in
1930, when she made her historic flight to Australia, and it
was from there that Imperial Airways pioneered
long-haul flights to the Empire.

When the Second World War broke out in 1939, the
RAF again took over Croydon, and it became one of the
star fighter bases, along with Biggin Hill and Kenley, for
the Battle of Britain. As such, it soon became the target for
enemy air attacks – it was bombed and strafed several
times. During one such raid, in August 1940, over sixty
people were killed and nearly 200 injured.

At the end of the war, it soon became obvious that, with
the rapid increase in air traffic, the size of aircraft and the
new jet liners, Croydon's days were numbered and in 1959
the airport was closed down.

In 1968, following a great deal of debate and argument
as to its future, the Roundshaw Housing Estate was
officially opened on part of the old Croydon Aerodrome.
This huge development, which consisted of some 1,800
houses, four schools, a health centre, library, shopping
centre and community building, became one of the most
controversial in Britain. But that is another story.

Heating for the houses was supplied by a massive
oil-fired boiler, housed in a large glass-fronted building on
the corner of Mollison Drive. It was one of the first
buildings to be completed on the site of one of the former
airport runways and only yards from where the RAF
personnel were quartered during the war. During the
commissioning of the boiler, construction workers
sleeping in the building were often wakened by the
inexplicable sounds of community singing and various
other noises, some of which are still heard to this day. One
of the council workmen was removing some rubbish at
about 6.30 one warm summer morning in 1971 when he
was astonished to see a motor-cyclist roar round the boiler
house and shoot past him at incredible speed. Nothing
unusual in these days – except that the motor-cycle made
no sound, and the rider had no face.

Theory has it that the unknown motor-cyclist is the

ghost of one of the 'few' who was killed when his aircraft crashed at the end of the runway during the Battle of Britain. The mysterious community singing is thought to be that of a ghostly ground crew who, during the long hours of the air raids of August 1940, were cheering themselves up with a sing-song in one of the staff huts which received a direct hit, blowing them to smithereens.

RAF Lindholme at Hatfield, near Doncaster, is said to be haunted by a big man in aircrew uniform. The spectre first made its appearance in 1947, when a group of airmen returning to the base saw the figure of a man walking out of the nearby marshes. He soon became known as 'Lindholme Willie' by airmen and locals alike, several of whom have seen him in recent years.

The villagers of Hatfield believe the ghost to be that of an airman killed in a crash on the marshes during World War II, and every description of him has been the same. In November 1957 a corporal in Air Traffic Control at the base reported seeing 'Willie' as his misty shape walked on the runway, having come from the direction of the marshes. Knowing an aircraft was due to land and thinking that someone had strayed onto the runway, he radioed control to alert them, but before he could take a closer look, the figure had vanished.

A sighting of a similar nature was experienced by ten-year-old Lee O'Hagan as he was being driven across Broughton Moor in Cumbria by his next-door neighbour, one bright summer day. Lee told me, 'I was looking at nothing in particular, when suddenly a figure loomed up in the road directly in front of the car.' The driver saw it at the same time and braked hard to avoid hitting what he at first thought was a hitch-hiker. Lee continued: 'I didn't know until much later that I had, in fact, seen a ghost. He wore what I later learned was the wartime uniform of a German Luftwaffe pilot, and this was thought to be the ghost of one of them, shot down over what had been a wartime ammunition dump.'

The tank museum at Bovington Camp in Dorset is

haunted by a German tank commander, known by the locals as 'Herman the German'. His haunt is centred around a German World War II Tiger tank on display at the museum. On numerous occasions he has been seen at the windows of the tank museum, staring out from the darkened interior. These windows are so high up in the walls that it would be impossible for humans to stand there.

At other times he has been spotted roaming around the camp itself, often gliding in total silence, almost indistinguishable in his blue-grey uniform. Sometimes he is heard but not seen, marching with heavy measured footsteps along the paths of the camp. Stories of the ghost are sufficiently detailed as to make night guard duty in the vicinity of the tank museum extremely unpopular, particularly on cold dark and windy nights.

Another military camp, at Tidworth Pennings, which lies north-east of Salisbury on the A338, has a ghost known to thousands of former troops for several decades, who has been nicknamed 'Scottie'. A huge ghost of a man over six foot tall, he is often seen standing on the skyline at dusk or on days when mist or rain obscures the hills.

The nickname was given to the ghost during the First World War, because he appears to be wearing a kilt, but it is thought he may, in fact, be the ghost of a Roman soldier, wearing not a kilt but a tunic. Theory has it that he was probably killed in a battle in the area some 1,900 years ago.

Several years ago he put in a remarkable appearance and was seen by several regular soldiers at the same time. A weapons demonstration was being held on an overcast day, when tracers could easily be seen in order to show the trajectory of the bullets. Right in the middle of the demonstration, the firing ceased. After a short time, an officer walked across to the NCO in charge and asked what was wrong. He was told that a figure in a kilt had begun to walk across the target area. As the men watched, the figure disappeared from sight in a bare area of clipped grass, with targets and a protective wall as a background.

One minute he was there, the next he had just faded away into thin air.

It seems that there is some truth in the old World War I song after all: 'Old soldiers never die, they simply fade away!'

4. Uneasy Lies the Head ...

It can happen to anyone, anywhere, at any time – the sudden chilling realization that you are seeing a ghost. Traditionally, phantoms are associated with haunted castles and gloomy old mansions, and even our Royal Family are not immune. Her Majesty the Queen is well aware of the truth of the saying 'Uneasy lies the head that wears the crown', for the troubled spirits of many of her predecessors still haunt several of the historic royal homes.

Althorp Park, in Northamptonshire, where Diana, Princess of Wales was brought up, is the family home of the Earl and Countess Spencer, and they are haunted by the ghost of a former servant, often seen in both the house and the grounds.

One witness of the haunting was Archdeacon Drury. In 1867, after a late game of cards with Lord Lyttleton, the two men were escorted to their respective rooms by a servant, who lit their way. Before bidding them goodnight, he respectfully reminded them to make sure they extinguished their candles, as Earl Spencer had a phobia concerning fire caused by carelessness.

Tired after a long and busy day, the Archdeacon soon fell fast asleep, but not long afterwards he was wakened by a light shining on him. The light came from a lantern held by a man standing at the foot of the four-poster bed – a man dressed in a striped shirt and cap. Angry at being wakened, the Archdeacon demanded to know the meaning of the intrusion, but he got no reply. The stranger simply lowered the lantern and walked slowly into the dressing-room, which later proved to have no other exit.

At breakfast, the Archdeacon mentioned the intruder to Lady Lyttleton, suspecting it had been a drunken servant. Gravely she informed him that what he had seen had been the ghost of one of Earl Spencer's faithful footmen who had died a few weeks earlier. It had been his responsibility to ensure that no candles or lamps had been left burning after everyone had retired for the night.

The same phantom servant has been seen in recent years in the grounds of Althorp Park, by a tourist who hoped to get a view of the famous household. He spotted what he took to be one of Earl Spencer's men, dressed in rough corduroy trousers and a striped shirt, leaning against a tree. The tourist called to the man, asking if it was possible to look over the house. He was annoyed at not getting a reply, concluding that the man was either insolent or deaf.

Shortly afterwards, he came across another estate worker who informed him that the house was not open to the public. The tourist could not restrain himself from complaining about the rude behaviour of the other man, but he was even more puzzled when he was told there were no other estate workers around at the time – they were all busy in the stables. When the tourist insisted and went on to describe the rude man, the worker went white with shock and in a shaking voice explained that the description perfectly fitted that of a long-dead servant.

HM The Queen has been reported as having seen the phantom figure of John Brown, confidant and, some say, lover of the widowed Queen Victoria, drifting around Balmoral Castle. He has been reported several times stalking the castle corridors and entrance hall – a magnificent sight in his kilt.

The ghost of Queen Victoria has been seen at Osborne House, on the Isle of Wight, the Queen's home during her latter years. Her ghost has been reported having been seen many times in recent years, usually walking slowly in the ground overlooking the Solent. In 1980 an American tourist claimed to have seen Victoria's ghost resting on an iron seat under an oak tree.

Princess Margaret's home, Kensington Palace, has a long and tragic history stretching back almost 300 years and is known as 'Hoodoo House' by the Royal Family. It was bought by William III for £200,000, and he narrowly escaped being burned to death there. William's wife, Mary, died there of smallpox at the age of thirty-two, and he too became a victim of the hoodoo, when he died there in agony, in 1702, following a fall from his horse.

Following the death of William and Mary, Queen Anne and Prince George moved in, but they had hardly unpacked when Prince George died, leaving her a widow at forty-three. Five years later, she too succumbed and died there of a mysterious illness. It was here too that George II dropped dead. (Actually George II suffered from painful piles and died after falling off the lavatory in 1760.) It was here that the Princess Sophia, daughter of George III, went blind, and her ghost is said to sit working at a spinning-wheel.

A man in white buckskin breeches has been seen strolling in the courtyards and on the roof: King George II has been reported, staring at the weather vane, waiting for favourable winds to bring ships bearing despatches and news from his beloved Hanover, all he had to look forward to in his old age.

For years, Sandringham House has played host to a mischievous Yuletide ghost, which generally livens up the Christmas celebrations, at least in the servants' quarters. This invisible phantom throws Christmas cards about, rips the sheets from newly made beds and terrifies the maids by breathing heavily in their ears!

Once, while staying at Sandringham as a guest, Prince Christopher of Greece – uncle of the Duke of Edinburgh – claimed to have seen the ghost of a mysterious woman wearing a mask. He said he glanced up from his book and saw her head and shoulders framed in the dressing-table mirror. He later described her as having soft, curly brown hair, a dimple in her chin and a ball mask over her eyes.

Later, on a visit to Lord Cholmondely's home, nearby Houghton Hall, Prince Christopher discovered who she was. He saw a portrait of the same woman, carrying a mask and wearing the same dress he had seen in his mirror. It was Dorothy Walpole, unhappily married in the eighteenth century. Her ghost was first reported as being seen by King George IV in 1786.

Buckingham Palace has at least one ghost, that of Major John Glynne, private secretary to King Edward VII, earlier this century. Fearing that mention of his name in a divorce case had brought dishonour on the Royal Family, he shot himself in his first-floor office. It is there that his shadowy spectre has often been seen since.

Gatcombe, the Cotswold home of the Princess Royal and her husband, Captain Mark Phillips, is said to be haunted by a huge black dog. Locals call him 'the Hound of Odin', saying that he is named after the god of the Vikings who plundered and pillaged Gloucestershire over a thousand years ago and who was always accompanied by a fierce four-legged fiend.

A ghastly ghoul is said to haunt St James's Palace – the figure of a man propped up in bed, with his jaw hanging open over a slit throat!

This ghost has been seen quite frequently, since one night in May 1810, when Sallis, the Italian-born valet of the Duke of Cumberland, was discovered dead in bed. The Duke later told an inquest that, when he returned from a night at the opera, Sallis had tried to kill him, had failed and had subsequently committed suicide. He denied that he had killed his valet because he was being blackmailed after seducing the man's daughter.

Prince and Princess Michael of Kent seem to be encumbered with one of the most dramatic spectres – that of a blacksmith, who is usually seen once a year at their imposing country home, Nether Lypiatt Manor in Gloucestershire.

According to tradition, the blacksmith's ghost rides up to the house on 25 January each year, just to remind the inhabitants of the wicked treachery which led to his death on the orders of one of the original owners, Judge Coxe.

Although few people care to wait up to see him, it is said that on the stroke of midnight a pale-faced figure astride a grey horse rides out of the winter mist. As he nears the manor, the big gates silently open of their own accord. Then the spectral blacksmith circles the courtyard before seizing the phantom of Judge Coxe and carrying him off.

No one knows very much about the spectral blacksmith, but we do know quite a lot about the notorious Judge Charles Coxe who built the Manor between 1695 and 1702. He was a Justice of the Brecon, Radnor and Glamorgan circuit, a person in a powerful and privileged position, something of which he was proud and in which he could not allow himself to be seen as anything less than a stern and righteous defender of the law.

From the moment the blacksmith stood before him in the gloomy courtroom, the shadow of death hung over him. His crime had been a capital offence – he had stolen a sheep to help feed his family for part of the harsh winter. He could expect no mercy from Judge Coxe. However, it so happened that the judge needed the services of a good blacksmith. Nether Lypiatt Manor needed a pair of good stout gates, so he told the blacksmith that if he would make him a pair of gates, and if he made them well enough, he would stave off the execution. The agreement was made and the blacksmith bowed from the dock in surprise.

The poor fellow worked day and night until the huge gates were finished. He then presented himself at the Manor, where he respectfully requested the judge's steward that his master should come and inspect the completed gates, adding that he had never made a finer pair. The blacksmith was sure his life would now be saved.

Judge Coxe took his time, enjoying every moment as the blacksmith sweated and waited, agonizing over the work.

The metalwork was good, the blacksmith had beaten and shaped the gates well, but he had overlooked a small fault at the top of the right-hand one. Judge Coxe could barely conceal his glee: the gates and the man were his – and the blacksmith's body was still warm when it was roughly thrown without any ceremony into an unmarked grave.

With his last breath, the blacksmith had vowed vengeance, and indeed, not very long after these events took place Judge Coxe was found dead in nearby Toadsmoor Woods. It was presumed he had died of a heart attack.

Publicly, Princess Michael takes a common-sense view that the story is merely a colourful legend. She was reported as saying, shortly after moving into the Manor, 'Ghosts are a lot of nonsense.' But is she really so convinced? Every year on the anniversary of the blacksmith's death, the Kents stay away from the Manor. And the author has it on good authority that they have also attempted to have the spirit exorcized.

Hampton Court Palace, that beautiful former royal residence alongside the River Thames, was given to King Henry VIII by his disgraced Chancellor, Cardinal Wolsey. One of the most famous ghosts to be encountered there is that of Queen Katherine Howard. She has been seen on so many occasions and by so many people that her ghost is officially recognized in the tourist guides.

Katherine married Henry VIII in 1541. She was a cousin of Anne Boleyn, a granddaughter of the second Duke of Norfolk, and was a lush, attractive girl on whom Henry doted and whom he once described as 'My rose without a thorn'. Little did he dream of the scandalous youth Katherine had spent in the disorderly home of the old Duchess of Norfolk, where, unknown to Her Grace, Katherine indulged in fun and frolics with various young men of the household. Before her marriage to Henry, she had been a little too free with her favours, having passionate love affairs with a variety of men, from page-boys to spinet teachers. Her reputation for immorality was the talk of the Court and, when she became Queen, it was difficult to conceal it from the King.

Henry was distraught and was said to have spent much of his time weeping. But even so, this did not prevent his sending her to the block, together with her lovers past and present. She had, after all, taken a lover after becoming his Queen and was therefore guilty of treason.

Young, vivacious and in love with her cousin, Thomas Culpepper, Katherine did not want to die. The story is told how, when she was arrested at Hampton Court, she broke away from the guards and ran along a gallery to the chapel where Henry – wily old fox that he was – with a typical touch of Tudor hypocrisy sat listening to Vespers and praying for her soul! Katherine hammered on the chapel door, making a last desperate plea for her life, but the guards seized her and dragged her screaming away from the chapel, while Henry pretended not to notice the disturbance.

Shrieking and struggling, Katherine was hurried from Hampton Court, put aboard a barge and taken down the Thames to the Tower of London where, on 15 February 1542, she went bravely to the block. However, her young protesting spirit returned to Hampton Court, where she is seen time and again, running frantically along that same gallery, her screams and shrieks chilling the bones of those who witness the spectacle.

At one time the haunted gallery was closed up, as a result of this invasion by Katherine's spirit. For a number of years it was used as a storage space for old furniture and tapestries, but in April 1918 it was again opened to the public and has remained so ever since. It appears that this had no effect on Katherine's noisy ghost, which, apart from being seen in the gallery, has also been seen in more tranquil fashion, flitting about the gardens of Hampton Court on sunny afternoons. Perhaps she is re-living the memories of more pleasant times before being sent on her sad way to the Tower.

Edward VI's mother – Jane Seymour – is also reputed to haunt Hampton Court Palace, where she died of puerperal fever in 1537, after giving birth to the sickly Edward. It has been suggested, a little unfairly perhaps, that her life was deliberately sacrificed by the performance of a Caesarean operation in order to ensure the safe arrival of the precious heir.

Jane haunts the Silver Stick Gallery and is said to appear every year on the anniversary of the birth of the baby prince, 12 October. Dressed in white, a lighted candle in her hand, she ascends the staircase leading to the gallery, where she then glides wreathed in a shimmering light, only to vanish when she reaches the far end. All this despite the fact that she had a most lavish funeral and that 1,200 Masses were paid for to ensure her soul had the peace of mind Henry considered it deserved.

Her Majesty the Queen is understandably proud of Windsor Castle, the royal retreat in Berkshire, and she delights in telling her guests about the castle's 'other occupants' – at least twenty-five spectral skeletons in the royal cupboard, sending shivers down the spines of her listeners.

It was at Windsor that Princess Margaret saw the stately figure of Queen Elizabeth I, the last Tudor monarch, who has wandered the twelfth-century castle since 1603. She is usually seen in the castle library, and it was here that she was seen by a number of people over the years, including an officer of the guard. He followed her into an adjoining room, but when he reached the door, Good Queen Bess had vanished.

King Charles I has also been reported many times, standing by a table in this same library, while George III, who died here in 1820 and was confined to the castle during the last years of his lunacy, has been seen and heard many times in various rooms, usually muttering that oft-used phrase of his, 'What, what?'

Another spectral nocturnal visitor to Windsor is the bulky figure of King Henry VIII. Some years ago, two guards saw him fade into a wall on the battlements. Later it was discovered that during Henry's reign there had been a door at that very spot.

Sentries on guard at Windsor have often seen the ghost

of a young guardsman who killed himself in 1927. Many who have seen him say he is so real-looking that they took him to be their relief.

A Coldstream Guardsman, found in a faint in the Great Park in 1976, had experienced a very different ghost. He reported later that he had seen Herne the Hunter, a man clad in deerskins and a helmet with antlers jutting from the forehead. Henry VIII claimed to have seen this ghost, and over the past 250 years there have been numerous reported sightings of the ghost of Richard II's forester, silently speeding through the castle grounds with his pack of spectral dogs. When the tree from which Herne the Hunter allegedly hanged himself was cut down in the 1860s, Queen Victoria reserved the logs for her own fire to help lay the ghost. It does not appear to have worked, for the sightings continue to this day.

In the seventeenth century, a terrified servant approached one of the castle guests, Sir George Villiers, with an extraordinary story. He said he had had three visits from the armour-clad ghost of Sir George's father, the Duke of Buckingham. The ghost had told him in sombre tones that, unless Sir George mended his evil ways, he had not long to live.

Sir George Villiers laughed off the warning – six months later he was assassinated.

For all their ghosts, none of the royal castles and palaces ranks as the most haunted place in Britain. That title rests with an ancient fortification that kings and queens of earlier ages used for less civilized purposes – the Tower of London.

Her Majesty's Tower of London – to give it its correct title – with its legendary ravens and colourful Beefeaters, attracts several million visitors each year from all parts of the world. The Beefeaters tell some terrifying tales of the ghosts which have haunted what was once the most blood-drenched spot in England for more than 700 years.

The first ghost recorded here was that of St Thomas à Becket, a Londoner and Constable of the Tower before he became Archbishop of Canterbury. Seventy-one years after his murder, in 1170, Becket's ghost was seen by a priest, striking the walls with a cross, whereupon 'they fell as if hit by an earthquake'.

Later Tower ghosts have far more dramatic reasons for their haunting. Anne Boleyn, Henry VIII's second wife, is one of the most frequently recorded spectres, having been spotted by several sentries over the years. One even faced a court-martial on her account. The man was found unconscious outside the King's House one night towards the end of 1864 and was accused of falling asleep on duty. At the court-martial, he told how a strange white figure had drifted towards him out of the mist, a figure which wore a bonnet but which was devoid of a head. He said he challenged the figure three times, but as it continued to advance, he ran it through with his bayonet, at which a flash of fire ran up his rifle barrel and he fainted.

Two other soldiers and an officer told the hearing how they had seen the apparition from a window of the Bloody Tower, and after hearing that the incident had taken place just beneath the window where Anne Boleyn spent the last night of her life, in May 1536, the court-martial cleared the unfortunate sentry.

Anne had a horror of being executed by a bungling English executioner, and Henry VIII agreed to have one imported from France, bringing with him a French sword. However, once the execution was over, all niceties ceased and her headless body was hurriedly bundled into an old arrow chest and buried with almost indecent haste in the Tower chapel.

Sentries claim to have seen Anne's headless ghost pacing up and down outside the tiny church, and one night one of the guards noticed an eerie light coming from the chapel windows. He brought a ladder and peered inside, only to see a ghostly procession of ladies and knights in Tudor dress file slowly up the aisle, led by the figure of Anne Boleyn. When she reached the altar, they all vanished, leaving the chapel in darkness again.

The ghosts of three other ladies who lost their heads have also been spotted. Queen Katherine Howard, who was beheaded in 1542, has been recognized as she walks the walls at night. Margaret, Countess of Salisbury, re-enacts her horrific execution of 1541, when she was dragged to the block screaming and the axeman chased her round, missing her three times before finally severing her head; and the lovely little Lady Jane Grey, nine days a queen, who died here with great dignity in 1554, at the age of seventeen.

Two sentries recognized Jane when they spotted the figure of a woman running along the battlements near the Salt Tower in 1954 – the 400th anniversary of her execution. Exactly three years later she was spotted again on the Salt Tower, which is where she was imprisoned before her death.

In 1970 a young woman from Grays, in Essex, saw the figure of a long-haired woman, wearing a long black velvet dress and white cap, standing by an open window in the Bloody Tower. Round her neck hung a large gold medallion. From the description, it appears that without doubt this too was the shade of Lady Jane Grey.

Phantom men and children also roam the Tower. In 1890 a sentry nearly died of fright when he was on duty in the Beauchamp Tower. He heard someone call his name, quite clearly, and looking round saw, floating in mid-air, a red and bloated face, with a loose, dribbling mouth and heavy-lidded, pale eyes. He had often seen it in the history books and knew without any doubt that he was staring into the face of Henry VIII, 'with all the Devil showing in him'. He was so afraid that he ran from the tower – the face following him!

In 1916 another sentry reported seeing a ghostly procession pass him near Spur Tower. A party of men were carrying a stretcher bearing the headless corpse of a man, his severed head tucked in beside his arm – a practice used in the fifteenth and sixteenth centuries when bodies were returned to the Tower for burial after execution on Tower Hill.

The ghost of the old Duke of Northumberland has been seen so often, walking the battlements between the Martin and Constable Towers, that this is officially known today as 'Northumberland's Walk'. Sir Walter Raleigh was executed here in 1618, and his ghost has reportedly been seen by sentries, as have the ghosts of two little children, seen walking hand in hand in the Bloody Tower. They are believed to be the shades of the 'Princes in the Tower', Edward and Richard, who were murdered in 1483, so that their uncle could claim the throne of England as King Richard III. Many other ghosts are known to haunt this historic fortification: a monk, several unidentified figures and even the ghost of a bear from the old Royal Menagerie which was housed in the Tower until 1843.

It is curious that there have never been reports of ghostly happenings or sightings in the largest and oldest of all the Tower buildings, the White Tower, built by William the Conqueror – the very heart of the Tower of London. Many historical celebrities have been incarcerated there, often in terrible conditions, one of whom was Guy Fawkes, the man who tried to blow up James I in the Houses of Parliament – yet, for some reason, none of them appears to have returned to the scene of their ordeal.

One clue as to why this may be so was uncovered in the 1850s, when masons were restoring the walls. When work on the White Tower began, in the eleventh century, it was believed that buildings could be protected against evil spirits by sacrificing animals in them. Eight hundred years later, the masons broke into one of the thickest stone walls – and found the mummified remains of an ancient cat!

How often, and for how long, do these unquiet spirits who lived in times past manifest themselves in times present – even times future? Are these spirits, sometimes tormented, sometimes benign, doomed to walk the royal residences forever? No one knows – not even Her Majesty The Queen.

5. The Stately Ghosts of England

It has often been said that there is nothing in the world to compare with the English stately home. One quality which houses of this kind have in abundance – and almost exclusively – is that the same families have lived in many of them for generations, for hundreds of years, in one case over 800 years. This means, of course, that they contain the leavings of several past black sheep. These houses were not just quiet backwaters; they are places where things have happened, where the future of Britain was discussed and often decided in the galleries and withdrawing-rooms. They were places of intrigue, treachery, greed and jealousy, so they also contain all the ingredients of a good haunting.

Bisham Abbey, near Marlow in Buckinghamshire, is a Tudor house which has long been reputed to be haunted. An abbey formerly occupied this site, and the mansion which now remains is pretty much as it was when King Henry VIII gave it to his former Queen, Anne of Cleves. Following Anne's death, the property passed into the hands of Sir Thomas Hoby, the man who was responsible for the custody of Princess Elizabeth during the reign of Queen Mary Tudor. Old Sir Thomas must have been a lenient jailor, for after her accession Queen Elizabeth I appointed him Ambassador to France. It is the tormented spectre of his wife, Lady Elizabeth, that has long haunted the house.
    For nearly 400 years, her ghost, dressed in mourning clothes, has been seen wandering the house and grounds, seemingly washing blood from her hands in a bowl which,

without any visible means of support, floats in front of her. Two schoolboys claim to have seen her sitting in a rowing-boat on the River Thames, which flows at the foot of the picturesque mansion's lawns. Both she and the boat vanished as the boys approached. There have been reports in the past of visitors being woken up in the middle of the night by the sound of footsteps shuffling along corridors – corridors which no longer exist! Sometimes the sounds of hysterical weeping are heard.

The ghost, which has been seen repeatedly over the centuries, is recognized as Dame Elizabeth from an old family portrait which still hangs in the Great Hall. She is represented with a very white face and hands and is dressed in the coif, weeds and wimple of a knight's widow. Strangely, all those who have seen her say that she appears like a photographic negative, with black face and hands and a brilliant white dress.

Towards the end of the nineteenth century, Admiral Vansittart was the owner of Bisham Abbey. He ridiculed the idea that there were such things as ghosts, but one night, after staying up late playing chess with his brother, he had an experience which was to change his mind completely. He later wrote: 'We had finished playing and my brother had gone to bed. I was standing alone in the Great Hall where Dame Hoby's portrait hangs. Suddenly, I felt that someone was standing behind me and I spun round, just in time to catch a glimpse of the spectral Dame. When I looked round to check her description from the portrait, the frame on the wall was empty!'

Dame Elizabeth Hoby was a close friend of Elizabeth I. She was a scholar who wrote poetry in both English and Latin and composed various religious treatises. She was also over-ambitious for her children, forever urging them to greater efforts in their studies. She despaired of William, her youngest son, a stupid child who, one historian says, died at an early age of a brain disease, aggravated by his mother's repeatedly boxing his ears because she had no patience with his dull wits.

However, there is a more colourful story, which received a certain amount of credence by a discovery made in 1840.

William, it is generally agreed, was a slow learner. Not only that: his exercise books were full of ungrammatical sentences, misspelt words and ink blots. His intolerant mother gave him several beatings which did nothing to improve his work. One morning Dame Elizabeth was particularly exasperated. She cuffed the boy round the ears and ordered him to repeat the work he had done so badly, locking him in a cupboard until he had completed the task. At this point a messenger arrived from Queen Elizabeth. She wanted Dame Elizabeth at Court immediately. The mother left in a hurry, forgetting to tell her servants where William was. When she returned home that evening, the boy was found dead, slumped over his books. Until her dying day, in 1609, Dame Elizabeth Hoby never forgave herself, and her spirit has roamed Bisham Abbey in remorse ever since.

In 1840 some alterations were carried out at the house, and workmen are said to have discovered some antique copy-books pushed into the wall between the joists and the skirting, beneath a sixteenth-century window-shutter. Several of the books contained a child's handwriting, and they bore the name of William Hoby on the covers. Several of them were indeed covered with ink blots – and one of the pages was blotted not with ink but with the stains of long-dried tears!

Alton Towers, formerly the home of the Talbot family, lies about six miles to the north of Uttoxeter in Staffordshire. It stands on a thickly wooded hill overlooking the Churnet Valley and is thought to be on the site of what may be the remains of an Iron Age encampment. Today the grounds are open to the public, and there are a great many facilities for children's recreation. There is an extensive fairground, rock gardens, fountains, bridges and ornamental gardens in abundance. In fact, today Alton Towers caters for almost everyone, and visitors go for a day out there in their thousands.

Some sixty years ago, Alton Towers was a different place, for the Talbot family – the family name of the Earls of Shrewsbury – were still in residence. One of their estate workers had an unusual experience which has never been properly explained. At the time he was engaged to be married and he had just seen his fiancée off on the train. In those days, a railway station stood on the south side of Alton Towers, the track running parallel to the river for some distance. (Although the rails are now long gone, it is still possible to make out their route.)

The way back to the big house was by way of what was known as the 'Step Walk', a path which winds upwards through the heavily wooded part of the grounds and contains some eighteen flights of steps, each flight having about ten or twelve steps.

It was sometime after 9.30 on a warm summer evening as the estate worker made his way back along this route. He had walked the path many times, by both day and night, and he knew it like the back of his hand. Between each flight of steps, there is a distance of several yards and, as he approached the final flight, he saw someone standing right at the very top, some thirty yards away from him. The estate worker took little notice of the stranger at first, assuming it was a guest from the house taking a stroll in the warm evening air. As he approached, the figure began to descend the steps and the worker could not help but notice his clothing and how shiny his shoes were – like patent leather. He was wearing a top hat and a long, flowing black cape. A white silk scarf hung round his neck and he carried a black, silver-topped walking-cane.

As the figure drew level with the estate worker, the latter touched his cap with a courteous 'Good night, sir.' As soon as he had uttered the words, the figure vanished. The young man stopped dead in his tracks. He looked round for the figure he had spoken to, but there was no one there, nor was there anywhere he could have hidden in such a short time. Feeling the hair at the back of his neck begin to bristle and an icy chill creeping down his spine, the estate worker ran home as fast as he could.

The following day he discussed his experience with the foreman, an elderly man who had worked on the Alton Towers estate for many years. He asked the surprised young man if the figure had been accompanied by a black dog. The younger man said that he had not noticed a dog, to which the old foreman replied that he too had seen the figure on several occasions, but each time there had been a black dog with it. He said that this was the result of an incident which took place late in the nineteenth century at the very spot where the figure was usually sighted.

It appears that there had been a party at Farley Hall, a large house which stood not far from Alton Towers. A guest had walked from the Hall to the Towers, where he was being accommodated. The following morning his body had been discovered at the top of the last flight of steps on the 'Step Walk', where he had apparently collapsed and died of a heart attack, brought on no doubt by climbing the steep 'Step Walk'.

Over the years the spectre has been seen several times by a variety of people, often accompanied by a black dog. But still, no one appears to know who he was – or why he should be seen going down the steps, when he apparently died after coming up them!

Sawston Hall, near Cambridge, is of Tudor origin, although remains of earlier occupation of the site include Roman and Saxon evidence. For 450 years it has been the ancestral home of the Huddlestons, a Roman Catholic family caught on the wrong side of the power-struggle for England following the death of King Henry VIII.

In 1553, before she became Queen of England, Mary Tudor spent a night in the Tapestry Room at Sawston Hall, and today the bed in which she is said to have slept is one of the highlights of the many exhibits displayed there. (Historically speaking, there is some doubt as to whether Mary actually did sleep in the Tapestry Room, but it is possible that the bed survived the fire referred to later in the text.) While she slept, Mary's weakling brother King Edward VI died, and before the news reached her, the scheming and powerful Duke of Northumberland tried to stage a *coup* by seizing the Tower of London, proclaiming his daughter-in-law, Lady Jane Grey, queen, and attempting to capture Mary Tudor. He sent her a message asking her to go to London to see her ailing brother, tactfully forgetting to tell her that Edward was already dead.

Somehow, her host at Sawston, John Huddleston, learned of the approaching danger in the early hours of 8 July 1553. He woke her and smuggled her out of the back door of the Hall, disguised as a milkmaid. Mary escaped just in the nick of time, with a few friends. On a hilltop, a safe distance from the house, they reined in their horses and looked back at Sawston Hall. The house was in flames. Unable to find Mary, Northumberland's men had set the place alight. Mary is said to have turned to her companions and said, 'Let it burn. When I am queen I will build Master Huddleston a finer house.' She was as good as her word: by removing the stones from Cambridge Castle, a noble mansion was built and completed in 1585 which still stands today, still inhabited by the Huddleston family.

Since her death on 17 November 1558, Mary's ghost has often been seen there, walking majestically in the grounds, as has the spectre of a 'grey lady' seen in the Tapestry Room, which survived the fire. The sound of a spinet being played was often heard until about fifty years ago, even though there was no such instrument in the house. I'm told that the music was not at all frightening, but that it sounded lovely and soothing. A few years ago, while helping to prepare for the opening to the public, the owner was alone in the Hall, waiting for the arrival of the young ladies who were to act as guides. Suddenly he heard the unmistakable sound of girlish laughter coming from an upper floor. An immediate search revealed no one there, and it was some time later that the guides arrived.

A clairvoyant once spent an uneasy night in the Tapestry Room. From about three o'clock in the morning he was wakened each hour by the sound of someone trying the latch of his bedroom door, and of footsteps walking about inside the room. This room is said to be haunted by a 'Grey Lady' who knocks three times on the door – which then opens of its own accord to let the apparition float in. A former maid once complained of being in the room when the 'grey thing' passed her. She was so frightened that she ran out of the room and fell down some stairs. Several visitors, sleeping in this same room, have reported that they were wakened by the sound of someone knocking on the door, followed by the sound of someone 'fiddling' with the latch. This would then be followed by a complete and ominous silence.

Another spectre said to haunt Sawston Hall is that of a watchman called Cutriss. Why he haunts the place is a mystery, but it is known that his descendants still live in the village.

Gawsworth Hall, on the A536 road four miles from Macclesfield in Cheshire, is the beautiful half-timbered house of the ancient Manor of Gawsworth, held by only five families since the time of the Normans. The house has witnessed many stirring events since the de Orrebby family first took up residence there in about 1130.

Gawsworth was the subject of the most famous duel in England, when in 1712 Lord Mohun fought the Duke of Hamilton and both contestants were killed. The 'Fighting' Fittons lived here from 1316 to 1622, and it is believed to be the ghost of Mary Fitton that today haunts the place.

Mary Fitton was appointed maid of honour to Queen Elizabeth I in 1596, probably as a result of her father's influence at Court. Unfortunately, her career was not to be a long one. In 1602 Sir Robert Cecil took it upon himself to inform Queen Elizabeth that the wayward Mary was pregnant. Elizabeth was outraged, sending Mary Fitton and her lover, the Earl of Pembroke, to the Tower of London, where they could 'dwell awhile until their ardour cooled'.

Another ghost said to haunt Gawsworth, is that of the eccentric eighteenth-century playwright and professional jester Samuel 'Maggotty' Johnson. He seems to have earned himself a place in immortality by having himself buried in unconsecrated ground, a local spinney known as 'Maggotty Johnson's Wood'. His unusual choice of resting-place is justified in verses on his tombstone, and his old violin – which is dated from 1771 – is preserved in the dining-room.

One of the more recent manifestations at Gawsworth Hall took place in February 1971, when Mrs Monica Richards, wife of the owner, reported the smell of incense occasionally creeping into her bedroom, which was situated immediately beneath a priest's hide. Here, some sixty-seven years ago, a skeleton was discovered behind a cupboard near an oratory which leads from the hiding-place and an escape hatch to the cellars. The bones were later interred in the churchyard, and the identity of the skeleton remains a mystery.

The smell of incense has been noted on several occasions, usually preceding the visit to the Hall of an archbishop. Once an archbishop commented, as he entered, on the thoughtfulness of the family to welcome him with incense – the family, in turn, thought the archbishop had brought it!

But it is the spectre of the gay and bright-eyed Mary Fitton for which Gawsworth Hall and its 500-year-old rectory are best known. One night the odd-job-man from the Hall was returning very late when he saw a cloaked female figure, which at first he took to be Mrs Richards. He raised his hat to her, but she gave no indication that she had seen him and carried on across the road.

At one time there was to have been a serious attempt to determine whether Mary Fitton was actually buried in Gawsworth church. Before the church authorities stepped in and brought the investigations to a halt, a coffin was located, which was bound with narrow leather straps decorated with a floral design. This was identical to that pictured in some portraits of this charming and promiscuous young woman who may have inspired Shakespeare to immortalize her in his sonnets. The 'Dark Lady' who today walks the courtyard and elsewhere in her ancient costume is thought to be Mary.

Still in Cheshire and not far away from Gawsworth, close to Jodrell Bank on the A34, seven miles south of Wilmslow, stands another grand old mansion, Capesthorne, thought to have been built about 1722 by John Wood of Bath. The chapel at Capesthorne is believed to be

the earliest surviving work of John Wood; the house itself
was later altered following a disastrous fire in 1861, when
much of the centre section was destroyed. It was
successfully re-built, and today there is hardly a trace of
the damage that was caused.

Of the many people who have experienced the
paranormal at Capesthorne, several have been Members
of Parliament. This is not surprising really, when one
learns that Lieutenant-Colonel Sir Walter Bromley-
Davenport, former owner of the Hall, was for many years
a Member of Parliament. Sir Charles Taylor, MP for
Eastbourne, was once staying with Sir Walter when he saw
the figure of a lady in grey float past, when he was about to
walk up the staircase in the west wing of the house at about
10.30 one night. He said that his attention was attracted by
the rustle of her long skirts coming from behind him. He
paused, looked down and saw the ghost floating along the
corridor. After a few seconds she was gone.

Sir Walter described how he had witnessed the same
ghost in one of the corridors leading from the
drawing-room to the dining-room, in what is probably the
oldest surviving part of the house. The figure's head was
bowed and she wore long and voluminous grey skirts – yet
she moved briskly and was soon out of sight.

Sir Walter's son, William, had the most frightening
experience one still night in 1958. He was wakened by the
sound of his bedroom window rattling. Jumping out of
bed to investigate, he saw what appeared to be a man's arm
reaching towards the frame. Quickly he strode to the
window, and as he reached the glass, the arm vanished.
The window was still shut and, on looking out, all he could
see was the empty moonlit courtyard over thirty feet below
him.

Sir Walter Bromley-Davenport had a unique experience
on 3 September 1968, the 250th anniversary of the
building of the private chapel. He went into the lovely old
chapel during the evening to check that everything was
ready for the anniversary service to be held the following
day. Suddenly he saw a line of about nine silent figures
descending the steps leading into the side of the family

vault. He called his wife, who at the time was in the library, but by the time she arrived the figures had evaporated into thin air.

There is nothing at all anonymous about the ghost which haunts the old Hall at Burton Agnes, which stands on the A166 between Driffield and Bridlington in Yorkshire.

Burton Agnes Hall, the seat of the Boynton family, dates from about 1600 and was built by Sir Henry Griffiths. Old Sir Henry had three daughters, and it is the youngest, Anne, who still haunts the Hall some 350 years after her death. Soon after the Hall was completed, Anne was attacked by footpads when returning from a visit to the home of the St Quintin family at Harpham. Her screams brought villagers running to the rescue, but she had been badly beaten and, although she was carried gently home and lovingly cared for, it was obvious she was not going to recover.

Just as a point of interest, some historians disagree and say that Burton Agnes Hall was itself under attack by marauding thieves and that Anne was mortally wounded in the struggle.

However, whichever way it happened, as she lay dying Anne made the extraordinary demand that her sisters cut off her head before burying her body, and preserve it in the walls of the house she loved. She warned vaguely of dire consequences if her wishes were disobeyed. Horrified at the idea, the sisters reluctantly promised they would do as she bid, though secretly they had no intention of doing so. Despite their promises to the dying girl, her wishes were not carried out, and Anne was buried in the yard of the old Norman church at Burton Agnes. A week later the trouble started.

First there was a terrific crash in one of the upstairs rooms. Seven days later, the entire household was awakened by doors slamming in every part of the building. Then the house shook with the clatter of heavy footsteps running along corridors and up and down the stairs, followed by a terrifying groan. The sounds went on all through the night, and the next morning several of the servants packed their bags and left.

The two surviving sisters called in the vicar of Burton Agnes. When they told him of Anne's dying wish, he agreed to open her grave. A shock was in store for them. When the coffin was opened, the head, already a grinning skull, was found to be severed from the shoulders, yet neither limbs nor trunk showed any sign of putrefaction.

Anne's skull was taken back to Burton Agnes Hall, and for a time all was quiet. Then one day a servant girl threw it out of the window, where it is said to have landed on a passing cart. The horses stopped, refusing to move an inch until the grisly relic had been removed. Since then, all attempts to bury it in consecrated ground have led to trouble. Over the years, several subsequent owners of the Hall have removed the skull, now known as 'Awd Nance', and each time mysterious shufflings and clatterings in the corridors, accompanied by slamming doors and terrifying groans, have forced them to restore it to its rightful place.

After being kept on a table in the Great Hall for many years, the skull was finally bricked up in a wall, where it remains to this day. However, the ghost of Anne Griffiths – 'Awd Nance' – still haunts the home she loved so much, apparently inspecting the furniture and making sure it is kept up to standard!

Bosworth Hall, at Husbands Boswell in Leicestershire, has a weird ghost that creaks and groans. It also has a blood-stained floor that has remained damp and sticky for over 300 years.

The Maxwell family have lived at Bosworth Hall for many generations, and the house has undergone considerable alterations in that time. But despite the twisting staircases and dark, rambling passageways, the Roman Catholic atmosphere of the place remains as strong as ever. During Cromwell's time, Masses were held here in secret, and one day Roundhead troopers were heard approaching, just as the family were about to celebrate such a Mass. However, they were prepared for such an eventuality, and the priest was hurriedly pushed into a hide, under the attic floor.

In his hurry to escape, the priest spilled the consecrated wine, or else — the true facts are uncertain — he cut his hand. In either event, the stain still marks the chapel floor, and to this day it still feels damp, as if it was made only a few minutes ago. So far no natural explanation has been given for it.

But the ghost of Bosworth Hall is not that of a priest. Lady Lisgar was a Protestant widow who in 1881 married Sir Francis Fortescue-Turville, and her shade is doomed to wander the Hall forever because she refused to allow a priest into the house to administer the last rites to a dying Roman Catholic servant.

A doctor, staying at the house, saw Lady Lisgar's ghost as he was on his way upstairs after dinner one evening. He passed a rather strangely dressed woman on the stairs, to whom he murmured a polite 'Good night', but received no reply. When he described the woman at breakfast the following morning, he was told, 'That was the ghost of Lady Lisgar. Please don't mention it in front of the children!'

The silent ghost has also been seen in the room where Lady Lisgar slept and where she died. She has been seen in the corridors, on stairways and in the passageways she helped to create, for it was she who carried out many of the changes at Bosworth. Guests complain that they are wakened during the night by fearful groans and unearthly creaks, and I'm told that one guest was actually thrown out of a four-poster bed with some force, landing on the floor with an agonizing crash.

Hurstmonceux Castle, near Eastbourne in Sussex, was built about 1440 by Sir Roger de Fiennes. No longer open to the public, it now houses the Royal Observatory. It also houses several ghosts.

One of the best known is that of a 'white lady' who has been seen swimming the moat. The story behind the ghost is that several centuries ago one of the de Fiennes enticed a local girl into the castle, where he tried to seduce her. The girl resisted his advances and tried to escape by swimming the moat. However, de Fiennes caught her and dragged her back to the castle, where she was raped and eventually murdered. (The bed in which the incident is said to have taken place has been preserved.) Since that night, the ghost of the girl has often been seen, soundlessly swimming the moat as if her life depended on it.

At the beginning of this century, Hurstmonceux was owned by Colonel Lowther, and one night he was crossing the courtyard when he met a girl whom he did not know. She was crying and wringing her hands, which, he later stated, where shrivelled and white. Thinking she was a gypsy begging, he went up to her, and as he did so, the figure vanished.

A second ghost, also seen by Colonel Lowther, is that of a man in riding-breeches and a velvet jacket. He was seen standing near the old bridge across the moat. Colonel Lowther was at the time mounted on horseback – and the figure walked straight towards him, passing through the terrified horse's head before disappearing.

Another ghost at Hurstmonceux is thought to be that of the young Grace Naylor, whose father bought the property in 1708. For some unknown reason, she is said to have been starved to death in a room in the east wing. She was buried in the family vault at nearby All Saints Church, but sounds of her sobbing and the occasional female figure are still encountered today, the figure floating along corridors and drifting through thick walls.

Georgina Naylor, a forceful and eccentric beauty who dabbled in the occult, lived at Hurstmonceux at the end of the eighteenth century. Dressed in a white cloak covered with occult symbols and with a white doe trotting at her side, she would ride each day on a white ass, to drink from what she said was an enchanted spring in the park. One day the doe was torn to pieces by a pack of hounds, and Georgina was so upset by it that she left Hurstmonceux forever, to live at Lausanne, where she died in 1806. For years afterwards there were reports of her spectre riding a white ass in and out of the deserted rooms.

Stories of Lord Dacre and a keeper have been told at Hurstmonceux for centuries, stories which probably go

Phantom Transport

Old Croydon aerodrome in the 1930s. During the Second World War, this was a star fighter base. Today, a housing estate covers the area, but the ghosts of some of 'the few' still haunt the site

Stockport boasted a haunted black taxi-cab. For some time it stood behind the premises of the taxi firm because no one would drive it!

Famous Ghosts

Queen Victoria's ghost was once seen by a tourist, sitting in the grounds of Osborne house on the Isle of Wight

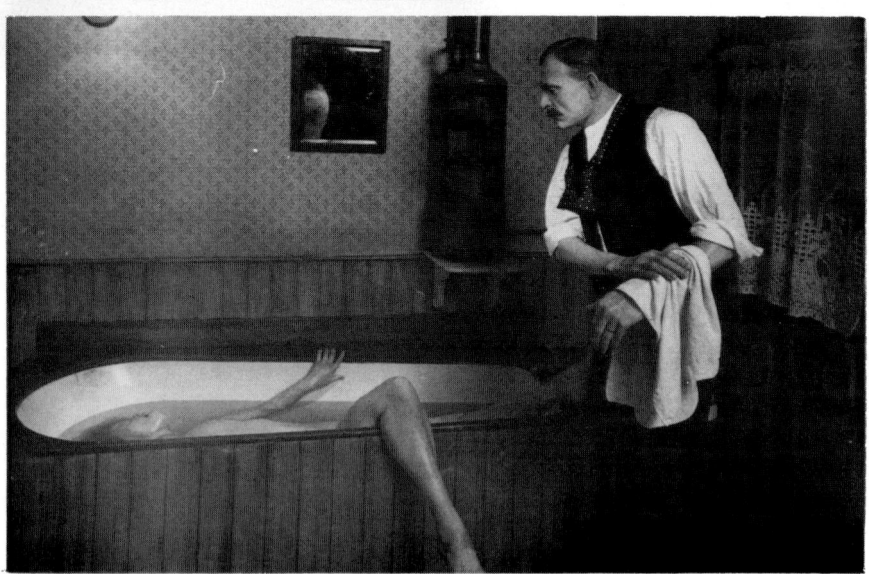

George Joseph Smith, the 'Brides-in-the-Bath' killer. A tableau at Madame Tussauds in London

Florence Nightingale – from the Tussaud exhibition at Windsor.
Her ghost was said to have been seen quite often at the Victoria
Military Hospital at Netley just before it closed

Haunted Palaces

The Chapel Royal, Hampton Court Palace. While Henry VIII sat at Vespers, his young queen Katherine Howard hammered on the door from the gallery outside, pleading for her life. The gallery is now said to be the scene of a ghostly re-enactment of the drama

St James's Palace, London. A ghastly ghoul, the figure of a man propped up in bed with his throat cut, is said to haunt the palace today

Kensington Palace, London. The home of HRH Princess Margaret, the palace is known by the Royal Family as 'Hoodoo House' because of the many tragedies in its 300-year history. One of the ghosts who walks here is said to be George II

Buckingham Palace, London. Haunted by at least one ghost, that of Edward VII's private secretary, who committed suicide in his office

London's Ghosts

The 'Dead Man's Walk', Newgate Prison. Newgate was a place of many ghosts, the best known being that of the wicked old baby farmer, Amelia Dyer

50, Berkeley Square, London. Now the home of Maggs Bros., antiquarian booksellers, this was once considered the most haunted house in London

The Tower of London. The Beefeaters can tell many hair-raising
tales of ghosts at this grim fortress

The Old Oak Inn, North End Road, London. Annie Doonan, a well-known prostitute, was last seen staggering drunkenly from this pub. The following day, her body was discovered in 'Second Hand City', where her ghost was often seen until the 'City' was demolished

Cockspur Street, London. Here a London taxi-driver saw the ghost of a headless woman glide in front of his cab, early one morning in 1975

Busby Stoop Inn, Northallerton. Several people have sat in Tom Busby's chair over the years, and have died shortly afterwards. Today, the chair has been removed out of harm's way

Maryport, Cumbria. The working men's club, where a ghostly
girl was seen to walk through the walls of the beer cellar

Chipping. Lancashire. 'Chilling' Chipping is said to boast more
ghosts than inhabitants. Perhaps the village's most famous ghost
is that of Lizzie Dean, a serving wench who haunts the Sun Inn at
the top of Main Street. Her body is buried in the churchyard
directly opposite the inn

Haunted Houses

The old windmill in Station Road, Wigton. Haunted by the ghost of John Chicken, the murderous miller

Chingle Hall, Lancashire, probably the most haunted house in England. Among the many ghosts here is that of a Roman soldier who was once photographed in the Great Hall

Borley Rectory, Essex, was once the most haunted house in England. It burnt down in mysterious circumstances in 1939, yet its legend lives on

Bosworth Hall, Husbands Bosworth. The ghost of the formidable Lady Lisgar, a nineteenth-century Protestant member of the family who refused a priest for a dying servant, is doomed to haunt the hall forever

back to the late fifteenth century when the young lord and his friends encountered three of Lord Pelham's keepers when on a poaching lark. A fight ensued and one of the keepers was killed by a blow from Lord Dacre's sword. Today it is said that the keeper haunts the field where he died and that Lord Dacre himself has been seen in the castle grounds, wearing a rust-coloured riding-cloak and large brass spurs and seated on a fine horse. I understand that he has been seen in quite recent years, but whenever he has been approached, he suddenly turns his horse and plunges into the moat, sinking in a cloud of mist.

As if all this was not enough to satisfy the most ardent ghost-hunter, the 'Drummer's Hall' at Hurstmonceux is also haunted by the ghost of a giant drummer, said to go back to the days of Sir Roger de Fiennes. This figure is said to have been seen striding along the battlements above the Great Hall, beating a drum and sending showers of sparks cascading from his drumsticks. The story behind this haunting suggests that a member of the Dacre family, who was supposed to be dead, lived on at Hurstmonceux in secret with his young and beautiful wife. In order to put an end to the young men who insisted in calling to pay their attentions to the young 'widow', he dressed himself in a drummer's uniform, smearing his clothes and drum with phosphorus and drummed his way across the battlements, thus scaring away his wife's suitors.

There are many alleged hauntings by the unhappy royal prisoner, Mary, Queen of Scots. Like Elizabeth I's, her ghost is said to pop up wherever she is supposed to have stayed. Few hauntings can be authenticated but some, such as the ghost that haunts the Turret House attached to the old manor castle at Sheffield in Yorkshire, can be authenticated by historical fact and eyewitness account.

The Earls of Shrewsbury held Sheffield Castle in the fifteenth century and when, in 1473, the third Earl died at the age of twenty-six, he left a son, George, who became the fourth Earl at the age of five. Young George was brought up by his guardian, Lord Hastings. In due course

he married Lord Hastings' daughter and took up
residence at Sheffield Castle, where he lived throughout
the reign of King Henry VII (1485-1509).

George, fourth Earl of Shrewsbury, was a man who
liked his comforts and he thought the castle too spartan by
far. We know the young Tudors liked comfortable living,
and George was no exception, preferring glass in his
windows, large, comfortable beds and chairs which at least
conformed to the contours of the human anatomy. He
therefore built for himself a more comfortable residence
in the castle park, which subsequently became known as
Manor Lodge. It was magnificently furnished throughout.
Two hundred and forty 'crowns of the sun' were spent on
wall-hangings alone. The forlorn remains which now
stand in Manor Lane bear little comparison with the
original, but the armorial overmantel and plaster ceilings
of the Turret House give some indication of the
ornamentation the house contained.

The Turret House was built by Earl Gilbert as a porter's
lodge, although many people still argue that it was
purposely built to house Mary, Queen of Scots. Evidence
shows that Mary was indeed held here as a prisoner, being
handed over to Earl George Talbot, grandson of the
fourth Earl, at Tutbury in 1569, and she was incarcerated
in Sheffield Castle itself on 28 November 1570. She
brought numerous retainers with her, but on the orders of
Queen Elizabeth I their number was cut down to thirty.

Now the castle became a prison, not only for the Scottish
Queen but also virtually for the young Earl and his wife,
Bess of Hardwick, whom he had married in 1568. The
slightest relaxation of vigilance and the royal prisoner set
about plotting her escape. In fact, it was as a result of this
that she was transferred to the Turret House, where
history records she was to spend nearly fourteen years a
prisoner of the Earl. However, in 1584 Earl George
petitioned Queen Elizabeth to release him from his
intolerable duty, and it no doubt came as a great relief
when she agreed and the unhappy Scottish Queen was
handed over to the custody of Sir John Somers and Sir
Ralph Sadler.

Mrs Ida Elliott of Sheffield spent quite some time at Turret House with her late husband's relatives, who, during the 1930s, were retainers of the late Duke of Northumberland, having spent many years in service on the estate. She told me: 'As I remember it, the place was quite gruesome, and my in-laws used to tell me some hair-raising stories of unaccountable happenings. None of them would stay in the place alone, day or night.' Mrs Elliott went on to say that on the Sunday following the Coronation of King George VI she was at Turret House, having been invited with her husband to have tea with his mother and an old aunt who lived with her. During the course of conversation the aunt said, quite casually, that she had seen the ghost of Mary, Queen of Scots, again, on the night of the Coronation.

No one but Mrs Elliott appeared the least bit surprised, but she sensed they felt a little uneasy when she pressed the old lady to tell her more about it. She was told that the aunt had been sitting up in bed drinking her cocoa when the apparition appeared, wearing a long black dress and looking radiantly beautiful. She glided across the room and evaporated into the opposite wall.

'As time went by and I got to know the family more, I asked if I could stay the night with them,' said Mrs Elliott, 'but I was always given a flat "no". When I asked them why not, the only reply I could get was that it was an evil house with very strange and disturbing things happening. People who had stayed there in the past had run out of the place in the small hours, refusing to go back, even in daylight.' She went on to say that she had later met someone who had stayed at Turret House, and she had been told that, although they had not actually seen anything, each time they were dropping off to sleep, they had the sensation that someone was trying to smother them and they had to fight off an unseen intruder.

During the 1930s Turret House was, unlike today, set more or less in open country, and to reach it one had to walk along a long drive. Apart from one or two farms and their outbuildings, it was surrounded by fields. Mrs Elliott said: 'My mother-in-law used to tell me that at twilight one could often glance at the window and find someone with feminine features, dressed in what appeared to be a cape and cowl, peering back at them. On going out to investigate, no person could be found. They soon learned to draw the curtains before lighting up the lamps.'

The house contained only six rooms. The two on the ground floor, partly oak-panelled with thick walls and iron-studded doors, had been the guardrooms during Mary's imprisonment. They were converted many years later into a kitchen and lounge. A stone spiral staircase led to two rooms on the first floor, which were used by the family as bedrooms. Two further rooms, unoccupied, made up the second floor, and these were thought to have been the rooms where the Scottish Queen was held. The stone staircase then continued up into the turret and led to a flat roof, which was the only place where Mary could exercise in the open air.

Mrs Elliott said: 'As I remember it, her sitting-room was quite ornate, with a magnificent fireplace. On the chimney breast was depicted her own coat-of-arms. The ceiling was of ornate plaster with various symbols and Latin phrases incorporated into it. The windows were diamond leaded and heavily barred, but in each diamond-shaped pane there was a red Tudor rose. These windows made the room very dark and dismal, and one could hardly see anything through them!'

One of the upper rooms contained an ancient incense-burner which had probably been in use since long before Mary's time to keep away evil spirits. Made from stone, it was about two feet tall and carved in the shape of an imp. Smoke from the incense came out of gaping holes where the eyes and mouth should have been. On a number of occasions, everyone in the house was wakened by unaccountable noises coming from this room, and fearing intruders, the men of the house hurriedly dressed and went to investigate, only to find nothing amiss.

One night, after being disturbed a number of times and finding nothing, the men were convinced that the old incense-burner had been moved to a different part of the room. After some discussion, they decided that perhaps they had imagined it but, to make absolutely sure, they drew a chalk circle around it on the stone floor, before once more returning to their warm beds. 'They were disturbed throughout the rest of the night,' said Mrs Elliott, 'but they ignored it until the following morning, when on investigation they found the incense-burner, which was far too heavy for them to move, was right outside the chalk circle!'

Turret House still stands, but it is now derelict and uninhabited except by rats and mice. Does the sad Scottish Queen still wander about the upper floors seeking solace or plotting escape? Or has she, like the estate, succumbed to a modern way of life which seems to have no place in it for antiquity?

We remain in the White Rose county for the next ghost in this chapter.

In 1934, a nineteen-year-old girl, whom to respect her wish to remain anonymous I will call Mary, went to work as a domestic maid at Nafferton Hall, between Driffield and Bridlington. She told me: 'It was in the middle of winter and, coming as I did from several miles away, I knew nothing at all of Nafferton or the old Hall.'

As was the custom with servants in those days, Mary was given a bedroom in the attic. The Hall itself had been converted to electricity by that time, but the cellars and the servants' quarters had not been connected and they still had to use candles. Mary continued: 'On going to bed on my very first night there, I had an odd sort of feeling. I can't say I felt afraid, more uncomfortable really. I did not like the scruffy room I had been given, and after a few nights I took the precaution of wedging a penknife in the door latch so that it could not be opened. We had no locks on our bedroom doors. One night I felt so uncomfortable, I lit my candle with my eyes shut, as I imagined there was someone in the room, staring at me in the darkness!'

Mary said that she had a strange, uncomfortable feeling whenever she had to go into the cellars, in particular the apple cellar. She hated having to go past there. There was a large stone slab set into the cellar floor with a huge iron ring in it, said to be the entrance to an underground passage. The door to the apple cellar was always open for some reason, and this too frightened Mary, who had to pass it each time she went to the dairy.

After being at the Hall for a few weeks, Mary became friends with the cook, and she told her of her feelings as regards to both the cellar and her bedroom. Cook told her that she had heard vague stories of a ghostly white lady who was supposed to haunt the Hall. Mary continued: 'Fortunately I never saw her, but somehow I got the feeling that she was connected with my bedroom in some way and that she was watching me whenever I was in there.'

The following summer, two young men came to spend a weekend at Nafferton Hall. They were university students and friends of the family, who used to invite them quite often. On this occasion they were to sleep in the empty room immediately beneath the attic room where Mary slept. She said: 'During the night I suddenly heard them jump out of bed and go racing downstairs. I heard a window open and then the chain and bolt on the front door began to rattle. All went quiet for several minutes before the window was closed and I heard the students come back to their room, where they talked animatedly for some time before finally going back to sleep.'

Serving breakfast the following morning, Mary over-heard a member of the household saying that she had heard the two students opening the door during the night. The students replied that they had not; they had gone through the window as it was quicker, and they had followed the figure of a 'white lady' across the lawn, where she suddenly disappeared. Mary heard no more of the conversation as she had to return reluctantly to the kitchen. She said: 'I gathered they had slept in that particular room with the intention of sighting the ghost of Nafferton Hall.'

Time passed and Mary was still unable to shake off the feeling of being watched. By the autumn of that year she had become very nervous and had decided to seek employment elsewhere. While she was working out her notice, she was alone in the house one afternoon, having been given strict instructions to have tea ready at a certain time, for when the family returned. When she began to prepare the tea she discovered there was no butter or milk in the kitchen and realized she would have to go down into the dairy in the cellars. Taking a candle, she set off into the gloomy cellars and as she passed the apple cellar door – which was again mysteriously open – she paused to close and fasten it. 'It fastened with a chain and padlock,' she said, 'although I did not padlock it, as that would have meant trouble from the family. I just put the chain over the staple and hooked the padlock through.'

Feeling less nervous with that door shut, Mary went on her way to the dairy. However, on her way back she nearly fainted when she saw that the apple cellar door was again open. She had not heard the chain fall, which she says she surely would if it had come open by itself.

The terrified Mary dashed to the kitchen, leaving her candle to burn itself out in the dairy, as she dare not, for the life of her, go back for it. Needless to say, she was in trouble when the family returned and the tea was not prepared. She was too afraid to tell them why. 'This is something I have regretted ever since,' Mary said, 'for, had I asked, I might have learned something about the ghost of Nafferton Hall. Perhaps I was too afraid to want to know at the time.'

6. Ministering Spirits

It is not only the stately homes of England which can claim to have their own ghosts; smaller houses contain spirits of the past, and among these the rectory seems to be a favoured haunt of many spectres.

The best known and most popular was, of course, Borley Rectory in Essex, about which far too much has already been written. Here was a good haunting which was exploited in the most cynical fashion, until it became history's most profitable ghost story. When Borley Rectory was discovered by Harry Price and Fleet Street in the 1930s, apparently there were not enough ghosts to satisfy those incorrigible publicity hounds, so others had to be invented. Thus what had begun as a genuine haunting was spoiled by the engineering of poltergeist phenomena, which has caused the cynics to dismiss the whole haunt as the biggest hoax of all time. That is sad, for, whatever the truth about Borley Rectory, it still holds one of the century's most interesting ghost stories.

It would be unwise of me to detail here the complete history of Borley, but basically the legend is that the rectory was built on the site of a thirteenth-century monastery and was linked with a convent a few miles away, at Bures. A monk fell in love with one of the nuns, both were caught before they had time to elope, and they were killed. Phantoms of the nun, the coach which she and the monk used, and a headless driver were all said to have been seen with alarming regularity in the nineteenth century.

Practically the whole thing was discredited in 1938, after Harry Price had rented the property for a year. He was instrumental in publicizing the ghosts and phenomena which he claimed existed there, through broadcasts, lectures and, more especially, his books. He claimed at one time that some 200 different ghosts existed in the old building!

The method of his investigation was severely criticized in 1956, when three members of the Society for Psychical Research carried out their own investigations. Their resultant book, *The Haunting of Borley Rectory*, suggested that Price had been guilty of considerable misrepresentation and that some of the so-called phenomena had been produced by him.

Unfortunately Price had died in 1948 and was therefore unable to answer his critics. Many people sprang to his defence, and another examination of the evidence in 1969 appeared to clear Price's name, but the damage had been done and grave doubts about the whole series of incidents still remain in the minds of many people. The building itself burned down in a mysterious blaze in 1939, and all that now remain of the original haunted area are the coach house and the parish church, opposite the site.

Council houses now cover the former rectory garden, but stories continue to be published which tell of a phantom nun still being seen, gliding down the 'Nun's Walk', usually on 28 or 29 July.

In the mid 1930s, just before seven o'clock on a warm Sunday evening, two young women were returning home to the then new vicarage which stands close to the church at Kingswood in Surrey. They were surprised to see a tall figure with his back towards them, standing at the gateway to the drive – a long, curving path that went round to the back of the house.

At first they thought it was the gardener, although he never worked on Sundays, and in any event he did not usually use that entrance. As they moved nearer, the figure walked in front of them up the driveway and round the house to a large oak tree. There it stopped and turned to face the girls with what they described as 'a queer loping step'. They described him as a tall man in a long, black, cassock-type garment, with a fringe of white at the bottom.

One of the young women later said that she felt her hair standing on end and wished that she could poke the apparition 'to see if it was solid'. It had a shock of yellow hair, but no face. It continued its unusual stride through a little gate at the side of the driveway and then silently vanished.

In the 1950s new occupants of the vicarage reported seeing the same faceless figure and said they had also discovered the back door of the house open on several occasions, despite its having been securely locked and bolted only minutes before.

There has been no real explanation to account for the appearance of the ghostly figure, but local suggestion is that it is the shade of a former gardener who, whilst up in the oak tree pruning some of the upper branches, accidentally fell off, badly disfiguring his face as he dropped to the ground. Other people put up a more reasonable argument in that they believe this may be the ghost of a leper who was brought to the household as an act of charity, by the first incumbent of the new vicarage.

About twenty years ago, there stood in the village of Maisemore, some three miles to the north of Gloucester, an old vicarage which was almost hidden from the road by high trees.

Under the house was a rambling old kitchen that had not been used for almost a century, but at times sounds that seemed to originate from that room suggested that people were walking about. One day the vicar went to see whether he could discover the causes of the noise and was surprised to find, standing in the middle of the floor of the old kitchen, the figure of a monk. When he spoke, asking if he could help in any way, the monk looked sadly at him, walked across the floor of the kitchen and, on reaching the opposite wall, suddenly vanished.

After this the vicar saw the monk several times in the old kitchen, but the figure always vanished a few seconds after being seen. It never spoke and always had a sad look on its face. Later enquiries revealed that once there had been a monastery nearby, but now only a few scattered stones marked the site.

One day the vicar noticed that the floor of the old kitchen appeared to be sagging, and so he sent for workmen to do what they could to repair it. When the workmen took up the floor, it was found that the whole flooring rested on two huge wooden beams which were almost rotted through with age and damp. Deep beneath them was a huge tank of water, which had possibly been the original water supply to the house in years gone by.

It seems the monk may have been there to warn of the necessity to have the floor joists replaced – for once the work was completed, the sad-faced ghost was never seen again.

In 1948 Canon and Mrs Wilfrid Garlic moved into the twenty-two-roomed St George's Vicarage at Otterspool in Stockport, Greater Manchester. They lived there for over a quarter of a century and for most of that time were haunted by the sound of footsteps which seemed to originate from an empty attic bedroom.

When they first became aware of them, both would be downstairs and in separate rooms, and each would assume that the noises were made by the other. However, on enquiring, it was always found that neither of them had entered the attic. They would then search the upstairs rooms for ages for signs of an intruder, yet each time they never saw anyone or discovered anything out of place.

Gradually they became used to the sounds of the phantom footsteps for which they could find no rational explanation, and in time they began to refer to them as those of 'the Archdeacon', after one of their predecessors, Archdeacon Thorpe – the formidable ancestor of former Liberal leader Jeremy Thorpe – who had lived at the vicarage from 1897 until his death in 1936. The sound was quite definitely that of footsteps, always seeming to come from the same place, but at different times of the day or night. The noises defied all logic – explanations such as water pipes, creaking floorboards, doors and windows rattling being discarded.

No actual sighting was made of any ghost, nor were the Garlics aware of any cold spots or temperature changes. In fact, there was nothing ghostly about the house and no element of fear. An interesting observation was made though. Sometimes the strange sounds would not be heard for several months, before starting up again, and it was noticed that the footsteps were heard most frequently at times of crisis for the Thorpe family. Apparently there was what was described as 'a real visitation' when Jeremy Thorpe's wife was killed in a car crash and when Archdeacon Thorpe's son-in-law died at sea. On that occasion the disturbances went on until a memorial service was held.

Canon and Mrs Garlic never found the noises disturbing, just curious. Once or twice other people claimed to have heard them also. From what I have been able to discover since, the footsteps have not been heard by succeeding incumbents, but I have learned that when Archdeacon Thorpe was alive the attic room where they seem to originate was the maid's room.

From 1937 to 1959, Langenhoe near Colchester in rural East Anglia was possessed of a haunted church and rectory, which stood side by side on a desolate landscape about a mile from the village.

In 1937 the Reverend Ernest Merryweather moved into the rectory, having exchanged his incumbency in the north of England for the grey, flat East Anglian landscape. In all his years in the north he'd had no experiences of the supernatural, nor had he shown much more than a passing interest in the subject. However, his removal to Langenhoe was to change all that, for within a few weeks of arriving he was to become involved in a series of strange events which were to last until his retirement over twenty years later.

At first the happenings appeared to be what can best be described as 'poltergeist pranks'. Doors in the church slammed shut in a violent manner, even on the calmest of days; the rector's briefcase locked itself, whilst on a desk in the vestry, refusing to open until it was well outside the building; flowers placed on the altar moved inexplicably from place to place or vanished altogether. Then there began thuds on doors, sharp cracks and the mysterious ringing of altar bells. Once Mr Merryweather heard the sound of an old man coughing – from the bricked-up doorway that had once been used as an entrance for the family of the Lords of the Manor.

In about 1947 the haunting took on a much more concrete form. Standing looking out his bedroom widow at the rectory and admiring the beautiful view, he was suddenly overwhelmed by the sensation of being embraced by a naked woman! Nothing was seen, heard or smelt, only the impression of soft arms, soft breasts and a body pressed up against him.

About a year later the female ghost made her presence known again. Because there had been an outbreak of hooliganism in which several people had been attacked, Mr Merryweather had taken to carrying a small dagger with him when he went into the church alone, purely for self-defence. One day, as he stood alone at the altar, he felt the dagger snatched from his belt, and at the same time a woman's voice from the other end of the church cried: 'You are a cruel man!'

It was in August 1949 that the phantom female made herself visible. During Holy Communion Mr Merryweather glanced up to see a woman aged about thirty, to all intents a living person, dressed in a long white dress with flowing headgear, move across the chancel and disappear through the solid wall of the south-west corner. Research later revealed that, prior to damage in the 1880s caused by a local earthquake, a doorway had once existed in that part of the wall.

In 1950 the ghost began a different approach, filling the church and rectory with an overpowering smell of violets, long out of season. The ghostly female was seen again in the rectory in 1951 and again in October 1952, and on one occasion, when the rector was standing in the vestry, he clearly heard a female voice chanting plainsong. About a week later he found two workmen nervously peering through the keyhole of the locked church and wondering how the sound of a group of people singing in French could come from what they knew was an empty building.

On another occasion, when Mr Merryweather was again alone and standing in the church entrance, he heard a muttered conversation in the chancel, with a man's voice raised but indecipherable. He dashed into the church to see who was there, only to hear a loud, unhappy sigh followed by silence.

Local tradition looks suspiciously like a story created to fit the facts – a woman murdered by some earlier rector who had become her lover. Some people claim that it was all in the mind of Mr Merryweather and that there was no haunting, although this seems rather harsh on the rector, who in his long life was always regarded as level-headed. The truth of the matter will never be known, for the church was demolished in 1962 and all that remained when I visited the site some years ago was a small field surrounded by gravestones which leaned at odd angles towards the empty space of turf in the centre where the church stood. The gravestones were overgrown with brambles, and the whole area gave the impression of an eerie sadness, silent except for the noisy rooks.

At the junction of Horn Lane and Western Avenue in East Acton, stands an old house, now St Gabriel's Vicarage, attached to St Dunstan's Church. This former farmhouse, with its cell-like cellars, cobbled paths and remains of a medieval courtyard, is thought to be all that is left of the once stately mansion of Friar's Place, built in the Middle Ages by the friars of St Bartholomew's at Smithfield.

Many people staying there claim to have heard uncanny noises, supposedly caused by the ghost of a monk buried under the path just outside the house – noises which sounded like padding footsteps on the stairs and in the hall, yet when anyone investigated, the place would be empty. A bedroom in one of the older parts of the house had a marble floor, and a startled guest sleeping in there was later to describe how one night he had seen the shadowy figure of a monk suddenly appear. The harmless spirit had, it seemed, returned to wander about what had once been used as an oratory.

The haunting was looked on with a certain amount of scepticism, more arguments being raised as to the actual age of some parts of the vicarage than over the ghosts, although it was generally agreed that, if the ancient monks had not actually lived on the vicarage site, they had certainly lived close to it on the land belonging to the church.

Late in 1946 a new vicar arrived, and he found that strange things were indeed happening, not only in St Gabriel's Vicarage but also in St Dunstan's Church. He recorded that, 'About a dozen monks can be seen on most evenings walking in procession up the centre aisle and into the chancel. They wear golden-brown habits and are hooded.' Another monk is often seen and was once seen celebrating Mass in the memorial chapel. He wears a violet hood belonging to a different religious order and is described as 'a ministering spirit'.

One night, when a discussion group was being held in the vestry, because of the warm weather the vestry door leading into the main body of the church was kept open, and witnesses saw a body of monks in brown habits walking in procession up the centre aisle towards the chancel.

It was inevitable that these events should come to the notice of the press, and in November 1946 the *Daily Graphic* sent along a reporter. His brief was to spend the night in St Dunstan's Church and either confirm or deny the story. In the event he was to experience more than even he had bargained for.

The reporter, Kenneth Mason, arrived at the church wet, cold and tired, and he took a seat in the far left corner of the nave. He said that the silence of the deserted church, combined with the heavy atmosphere of the place, forced him to drowse until he eventually fell asleep. Then, suddenly, he woke up with a start, not knowing what had wakened him. But as his eyes became accustomed to the gloom, he saw six phantom monks in greyish-brown gowns and hoods, walking slowly towards him, their heads bowed.

Kenneth Mason reported: 'Slowly but happily they came towards me. I took my courage in both hands and faced them, barring their way. Then quickly I had to turn and look back at them – they had passed right through me!' They were walking towards the altar and had passed through him two-by-two. Reverently the monks genuflected to the altar, and then at the back of the church a light snapped on and a human voice enquired if he was all right. The spell was broken. Kenneth said, 'From the tower came a mournful toll of the service bell and at its sound the monks vanished, while I was left wide awake, uncomfortable and wondering.'

These events took place at seven o'clock one Friday night. Over the weekend Kenneth returned to St Dunstan's with a staff photographer in the hope of obtaining a picture of the ghostly monks. Near the vestry door, a spectral monk stood looking on as the frantic photographer tried in vain to capture his image. Unfortunately the noise of several people trying to get into the church to see the ghosts for themselves upset the whole atmosphere.

It was a warm and pleasant sunny day in 1932 and in the small Devon village of Spreyton the Reverend W.R. Dunstan and a friend were out on the lawn, taking it in turns to photograph each other in front of the vicarage. The photographs they took with an inexpensive camera began a series of arguments that went on for years. On each photograph there appeared the shadowy form of a kneeling monk some five or six feet from the camera. He appeared to be at prayer, wearing a long flowing robe and hood. This was just one of a series of unusual occurrences which took place at Spreyton vicarage, a centuries-old building.

One evening, while discussing church matters in an upstairs room with the sexton, Mr Dunstan heard quite distinct footsteps cross the hall beneath him. They were calm, unhurried and deliberate, and both he and the sexton sat amazed, knowing that there were no other humans in the house at the time. As suddenly as they began, the footsteps ceased, and both men dashed downstairs to investigate, only to find the hallway empty.

On another occasion, the Reverend and Mrs Dunstan were in bed and sleeping soundly when Mrs Dunstan was wakened by footsteps crossing the hall, climbing the stairs, passing the bedroom door and going into the room next door, where some washing was airing on a clothes-airer. Suddenly there was a clatter which sounded as if someone had tripped over the clothes-airer and had knocked it over. The noise woke her husband and they both went to investigate – but as usual there was nothing, and the clothes were just as they had been left.

Often they would hear a chair or something fall in another room. They could tell by the sound exactly what had fallen over, yet never, on inspection, did they find anything out of place. Although the ghostly footsteps and other strange noises continued for a number of years, no apparition was ever seen at the vicarage, other than the one caught by the camera in 1932. Nor was there any real explanation for the haunting, despite tales told by other incumbents over the years. The only slender clue provided by history was that in 1445 the parish priest was a man called Henry de Mayne, whose name was a corruption of 'le moine', which is French for 'the monk'. However, this seems a very tenuous link to me.

Around Christmas 1932, news spread throughout Hereford that two policemen had encountered the ghost of a monk outside St Peter's Church. They reported that just after midnight they had met in the deserted St Peter's Square – at least, they thought it was deserted. One of them noticed a figure apparently leaning against the war memorial, wearing a dark, flowing robe. The policemen immediately thought it was a drunken Christmas reveller on his way home from some fancy dress party and approached him, as policemen do, to ask him to move along quietly. But as they got near to the robed figure, it slowly walked towards the main porch of St Peter's Church and, without even a moment's hesitation, walked straight through the massive iron gates, which they checked, only to discover that they were securely padlocked. The figure then proceeded on an eerie journey through the heavy oak doors of the church, which were also securely fastened.

The *Hereford Times* questioned the police officers, and one of them claimed to have seen the same ghost a few years earlier. When the article was published, other people began to come forward with similar stories, one of whom was the church organist, who claimed to have seen the spectral monk on a number of occasions. Despite these disclosures, the episode was not followed up and it soon faded from the public mind. However, late one night in September two years later, the city was the scene of ghostly activity of more sensational proportions, when the same two police officers saw a dark figure moving through the close of Hereford Cathedral.

Because of its dark appearance, one of the constables, thinking it was a colleague, called out a greeting, at which the figure immediately vanished – but not before the policemen had been able to take in details of its dirty robe and cowl.

A few days afterwards a man was walking through the close at about 2.30 in the morning when he saw a sudden ray of light move across a corner of the Deanery, and when he had walked on a few more yards, another light quickly followed it. There was nothing to account for the strange lights, and he was still puzzling over them when he saw a figure glide from behind a wall near the Deanery. Transfixed with terror, he registered every movement of the ghost. First he saw the upper part of the body become visible, as if it was cautiously peering round the corner, then the whole figure appeared on the path walking rigidly with its hands at its side. No face was visible, but it was possible to see that he was wearing a cassock and cowl.

Only about a week later, at about the same time, a courting couple were passing the close when they saw the ghostly monk, with his arms folded across his chest, glide across the close with the air of someone deep in thought.

These reports encouraged a group of people to keep watch, and one Sunday night a party of about a dozen men and women kept vigil in the cold close until the early hours. Shortly after midnight they took up their positions opposite the cathedral entrance and waited quietly. Their patience was rewarded two hours later, when all the group observed strange rays of light coming from the cathedral windows. Then, within a few yards of them, the bent figure of a monk emerged from the wall on one side of the close. The figure seemed to be crouching as if he was carrying something heavy, and it was easy to make out his cowl and dirty robe with a lace fringe, which covered a black undergarment. The figure stood out against the darkness of the night, yet it was not possible to make out the features of his face.

Not long afterwards, a man and his wife claimed to have seen the spectre near the library at the west end of the cathedral, some distance from the Deanery. First, they too saw a strange light flash across the library window, and this was followed almost immediately by a cowled figure which walked slowly, with its head down as if looking for something.

Over the years there have been dozens of alleged sightings, although at the time of the above incidents the Dean of Hereford Cathedral would not admit to the place being haunted and said it was obviously the work of a practical joker. But many Hereford people know better and remain unshaken in their belief that the shabby little monk was a ghost – and events so far have not proved them wrong.

Very early one cold dark January morning in 1964, two young women were cycling to their work at a newly opened Ford assembly plant near Basildon New Town, in Essex. Suddenly they saw the ghostly figure of a monk float across the road in front of them. They pedalled furiously, speechless and shaken, until they were well past the ancient Holy Cross Church, near where the spectre had appeared. This was one ghastly incident which neither of them wanted to experience again.

However, at about the same time several mornings later, the same ghostly figure, robed in a crimson gown, again appeared in the road directly in the path of their bicycles. Alarmed, one of the women rang her bell but the figure remained motionless and she rode straight through it. A few days afterwards, and without any knowledge of the phantom monk, ten women cleaners from the factory engaged on the night shift all saw the phantom monk while walking or cycling home from work in the early hours. They saw it in pairs, and they saw it individually, 'just floating in deathly silence'.

The monk seemed to come out of the bushes at the roadside, shuffled eerily and silently across the road and disappeared among the graves of the thirteenth-century Holy Cross churchyard. Over a short period dozens of women from the car plant saw the figure and were so terrified that they refused to use the road except in groups. The sightings were nearly always between four and six o'clock in the morning. The women's story was widely reported in the newspapers, and this brought reports from a number of local residents who were convinced that Holy Cross churchyard was haunted. The newspaper articles brought a constant stream of sightseers to the spot, causing nuisance to the local residents and damage to the churchyard.

At the time, the curate of Holy Cross Church was the Reverend B. Lloyd. He said that he had never seen anything strange, in either the church or the churchyard, although he did admit that when he had been in the church late on dark winter's nights he had often heard odd noises which he thought sounded like footsteps in the church porch, but he had put the noises down to things like bats and mice.

From the description the women gave, Mr Lloyd said that, if there was a ghost, it could be that of a former Basildon rector who became Dean of a London church – which would account for the crimson gown. He said there was no question of an exorcism, as such a ceremony could not be conducted on consecrated ground. However, all the interest and activity seems to have scared him off, for the crimson monk – or whatever he was – has not been seen, so far as I am aware, since 1965.

14 November 1956 is a date that will long remain in the memory of retired policeman Raymond Hawes. Ten years previously, Lord Amherst of Hackney had died and had been laid to rest within a short distance of his former home, Didlington Hall, in Norfolk. The Hall had been partly demolished by 1956, and only the old tower and two small cottages remained standing. This area of England is steeped in superstition, and most nights the Norfolk villagers told stories in the village pub about a ghostly coach-and-four seen driving along the lane leading to Didlington church. Strangers to the district listened eagerly. Some believed the yarns, some did not. One of the non-believers was the local beat bobby, Raymond Hawes.

It was 10.50 p.m. The wind cut across the lane directly down a forestry ridgeway, and his heavy blue serge uniform did little to keep out the cold. He reckoned that, if he rode his cycle slowly and gave attention to the farm premises along the way, he should reach Didlington church by about eleven o'clock. That would be his last round before passing on to one last parish to finish his tour of duty for the night.

At first he could not believe his ears. Was the wind playing tricks? He listened again, turning his head towards the sound, and realized that it was definitely the clanging of a bell. He thought it must be Didlington church clock chiming and then he remembered that the clock hadn't been working for years. He jumped on his bicycle and rode off in the direction of the church, the tolling bell pounding in his ears. There was no doubt about it: it was the church bell, and he counted at least twenty-five tolls.

He reached the lych-gate and the ringing suddenly stopped, as if his presence was known and whoever was ringing the bell had made a sudden exit. The silence was frightening. Only the wind in the trees could be heard. His mind in a whirl, Constable Hawes stepped onto the church path, rapidly running through all the possible logical explanations. A prank? Children? If not, what could possibly cause a half-ton church bell to swing? Certainly not the wind. By now he had reached the church door, which was locked. There was no key in the keyhole but he knew it was usually left under the doormat.

Slowly, making as little sound as possible, he turned the large key in the lock and the door creaked open, swinging to its full width. The constable flashed his torch over the pews, then under the belfry where the bell-rope would be. He saw the bell-rope and gasped – it was swinging backwards and forwards as if someone had just released it, yet there was not a soul in sight. A shiver ran through his body, his mouth went dry, and all he wanted to do now was to retreat as quickly as possible, for he had a distinct feeling that he was not alone, that someone was watching him.

PC Hawes was still shocked when he arrived home sometime after midnight, and the matter puzzled him for several days after. Then one day he was talking to an aged parishioner who had worked at Didlington Hall and he asked him, 'When did Lord Amherst die?' The answer was '14 November 1946' – exactly ten years to the day before the policeman had encountered the phantom bell-ringer at Didlington church.

And finally, if the reader should think that spectral monks, phantom bell-ringers and ghostly rectors are enough to turn the hair white overnight, spare a thought for one rector who lived in the fine old Queen Anne rectory at Ash, near Aldershot, in 1938.

The Reverend W. Blakey told in his parish magazine how he had suddenly been woken from his sleep in the small hours by the noise of a post-horn and galloping horses. The next thing, he was sitting up in bed, wide awake, when a ghostly coach-and-four clattered right through his bedroom, in the direction of the church. He said: 'No one was more surprised than I was, at being wakened by the sound of a horn and the thud of horses and seeing this unique apparition canter through the house. It was so realistic. I both saw it and heard it quite distinctly!'

The Queen Anne rectory was built on the site of an older coach road, and Mr Blakey thought that the coach-and-four, resenting the intrusion on its right of way, continued to drive through the old place as if it did not exist. On making further enquiries, he was to discover that previous rectors had also witnessed the same noisy passage of the spectral stage-coach.

7. Phantom Hitch-Hikers and Other Nasties

In June 1949 a family of four were travelling from their home in Stafford to Sussex, at the start of their annual holiday. They passed through Milford on the Rugeley road heading towards Lichfield just after seven o'clock in the morning. The road was empty, save for a man on a bicycle riding towards Rugeley, who came into view only after the car had struggled over the last rise near a place called Weetmans Bridge. The cyclist was dressed in a heavy black serge jacket and trousers, and he was pedalling along on a high-framed bicycle which, even by post-war standards, looked rather ancient. The driver eased the car towards the centre of the road instinctively to overtake and was just about to pass him when, to his absolute amazement, he saw the road was completely empty but for his own car. The solid figure, pedalling a solid bicycle, had vanished before his incredulous eyes.

Both the driver and his wife, without a shadow of doubt, saw the cyclist who in less than a split second just wasn't there. They were not the first nor the last people to see the phantom cyclist, for he has haunted the Rugeley road since earlier this century, when there was an accident during the construction of a water pumping station, still standing near Weetmans Bridge.

It appears that the local water company had drilled a deep, vertical bore-hole, and one morning, just after the men had begun work, one of the workmen fell down the shaft and was choked to death at the bottom. A fireman had to go down in a bucket to retrieve the body. Ever since that day, the stretch of road has had a reputation for being haunted.

Not far away, at Eccleshall, there is a stretch of road known as 'Ghost Mile' by the locals. Here many people have reported seeing the figure of a man, dressed in Tudor costume, glide across the road. On one occasion, a young man, driving along this road on a winter evening, saw someone dash out of the hedge, right in front of the car. There was no time to apply the brakes, and the car ploughed right into the running figure. The driver got out, expecting to find the twisted body of a man in the road – but found nothing. There were no marks on his car which indicated a bump and, on reflection, he realized that there had, in fact, been no impact. Who the Tudor ghost is, no one knows, but he has been responsible for a number of accidents on that stretch of road over the years.

The villages of Mildenhall and Axford stand on the B4567 between Marlborough and Hungerford, and in the 1870s an accident occurred on the road between the two villages which resulted in the death of fourteen-year-old Alfred Watts. According to local records, a team of horses panicked and ran down the hill, dashing the driver and the boy to one side in their efforts to stop them. The boy fell to the ground, and the wheels of the loaded cart ran over him, killing him instantly. Exactly opposite the spot where the boy died, a small memorial stone was erected in a cutting made into the bank at the side of the road.

One autumn evening towards the end of the 1950s, a party of four people were driving home following a visit to the cinema in Marlborough. As they approached the spot where the accident had occurred some ninety years earlier, the glare of the car headlights picked up, quite clearly, the figure of a tall, thin, clean-shaven man standing in the centre of the road immediately opposite the small memorial stone. The man wore a long, light brown coat, and his hair was grey; he was gazing intently, with his back to the memorial stone. Although he would have been aware of the headlights and the approaching car, he made no attempt to move out of the way.

At a distance of some fifty yards, the driver blew the horn, but still the figure did not move, nor even turn its head, and the car was forced to slew to a halt a few yards away. For a moment or two, the occupants stared at the stranger, surprised to find someone, apparently drunk, in such a remote spot. The driver opened the car door with the intention of remonstrating with the man, and suddenly all four people were looking mystified – the seemingly solid figure had simply vanished. One moment he was there and the next he was gone! It was impossible for a human being to have vanished so quickly up one of the banks on either side of the road. The four passengers got out of the car and searched both sides with torches, but nothing or no one was found.

Later enquiries revealed that Alfred Watts' father was a very tall and gaunt man who was clean-shaven and who characteristically dressed in white trousers and a long, light brown coat.

The ghostly figure was, to my knowledge, seen only a couple of times, and although there is no concrete evidence to suggest why he should have been seen at that spot, it is interesting to note that a few months after these events the memorial stone was dug up and thrown with other rubble on top of the cutting, when the county council widened the road. I understand that today a new memorial stone can be found by the side of the road, just a few yards away from the site of the original one.

Readers who can remember 1940 will recall how the year closed on a note of gloom. Britain had been pitched into a war which we seemed to be on the verge of losing; our troops had evacuated Dunkirk, Norway and Somaliland; the Luftwaffe had already made raids on London and Coventry and, to cap it all, the winter of 1940 was one of the severest on record, the whole of Britain being gripped in the claws of hard frost and blanketed in deep snow.

None of this, however, was going to stand in the way of George Dobbs when he made up his mind to visit his local pub, the White Hills, on the outskirts of Northampton. On arrival he discovered that he was rationed to only one pint of beer, and so he set off for another pub, the Fox and Hounds, about a half-mile further up the road.

Plodding earnestly through the snow up a slope leading towards the cemetery gates, he noticed a car lumbering towards him slowly, its wheels blindly following the deep frozen ruts in the snow. In petrol-rationed Britain, seeing a car was something of a rarity and he glanced up. Suddenly he saw, silhouetted against the dim headlights, a cyclist coming towards him and laboriously struggling to keep his balance as he moved forward, even more of a prisoner of the deep snow than the car.

As Mr Dodds turned back to his own problems of negotiating the snow, he suddenly realized that the cyclist had looked as if he had no head. 'It must have been a trick of the headlights,' he thought. 'The chap was probably wearing a dark muffler and a balaclava to keep out the cold.' Then, after a moment or two, it suddenly dawned on him that the car was not slowing down and that there was going to be an accident. Looking up again to see what was going on, he heard the car engine growling unchanged in low gear and saw to his horror that the vehicle was almost on top of the unfortunate cyclist, who was apparently desperately trying to keep his cycle upright and was totally oblivious of the approaching car.

Before he had time to collect his thoughts, the car was level with Mr Dodds, and without even a slight alteration of pace it crawled past, ploughing through the snow in the direction of Market Harborough. Apart from the noise of the groaning engine and the crunch of frozen snow, there had been no other sound. Thinking the snow could have muffled the sound of an impact, Mr Dodds hurried to the spot where he knew the car must have struck the cyclist. He reached the spot where he had last seen the man on the bike, crossing and re-crossing the road, but there was no sign of him. He searched the verges in case the victim had been thrown or had jumped to one side, but there was nothing, no wrecked cycle, no mangled body. Thoroughly scared, Mr Dodds raced as fast as his legs and the snow would allow him, to the Fox and Hounds.

The story he told in the pub was greeted with laughter and derision, making little impression on the regulars – that is, until one old man spoke up. He was one of the pub's oldest customers and had been for many years the local grave-digger. He said: 'That was old Harry Potts. I buried him about twenty-five years ago. There was deep snow at the time and he was knocked off his bike just by the cemetery gates. In the crash his head was TORN OFF HIS SHOULDERS!'

Spectral jay-walkers are common in England, as many drivers will testify. An old gypsy woman staggers across the Bath to Bradford-on-Avon road at a place called Sally-in-the-Wood, a notorious spot for vehicles plunging off the road. At Barrow Gurney, south-west of Bristol on the A38, several drivers have skidded to a halt to avoid hitting a woman in a white coat who suddenly appears, then vanishes.

Lorry-driver Laurie Newman spotted what he thought was a figure of a nun walking beside the A4 as he drove from Chippenham to Bath at about 2.30 one morning. He slowed down, intending to pull out and pass her, but as he did so, the figure turned and sprang, clutching the side of his cab and leering through the near-side window. Shocked, Laurie stared back – into the face of a grinning skull. Similarly Sebastian Cliffe experienced a highway haunting as he drove from Bath to Warminster. Approaching the bend at Limpley Stoke, all his dashboard gauges ceased to function and he felt a sudden chill. Suddenly a ghostly face appeared in his windscreen. As it slowly faded, so the gauges began to work again.

East Anglia police think that the ghost of a hunchback postman who died in 1899 has returned as a twentieth-century killer, following three deaths on a lonely country road, the A12, between Great Yarmouth and Lowestoft.

The first victim was a lorry-driver who knew the route well. Yet, for no reason, his vehicle careered off the road and smashed into trees, back in 1960. In 1980 a car-driver who was also familiar with the road drove crazily into the same trees. Within a year, a cyclist unaccountably swerved into the path of an on-coming car. In all three cases, the coroner recorded an open verdict.

Survivors of accidents on this stretch of road have claimed that a 'shadowy figure' forced them to swerve. One young man said that the figure of an old man was standing in the slow lane, just looking at him. 'I slammed my brakes on and skidded, expecting a thud, but the car went straight through him and hit the kerb!' When he got out to investigate, there was no sign of the old man. A former Lowestoft policeman claims he has seen a hunchback figure with long straggly hair, who just walked across the A12 and disappeared.

It is thought that this is the ghost of William Balls, a postman whose body was found in the area during the severe winter of 1899.

It was a ghostly figure which probably saved the life of driver Agnes Kelly of Huddersfield. As she drove her car into a sharp bend, the glare of on-coming headlights picked out the figure of a fair-haired boy. Horrified, she swung the steering-wheel over as the boy's freckled face loomed up in front of the windscreen. That single act probably saved her life. She crashed into a parked car but suffered only shock. As she waited for an ambulance, she anxiously asked a policeman, 'Have I killed the boy?' But there was no boy.

A court heard in January 1981 that what Mrs Kelly saw as she took the bend in Somerset Road, Huddersfield, was the ghost of an eight-year-old boy who had been knocked down and killed by a car on the same spot many years before. After the case she said: 'But for the figure of the boy, I am sure I would have driven straight into the car coming up the hill towards me. I most probably would have been killed!'

During the mid-1930s, a large red bus which bore the No.7 route number began harassing motorists in the North Kensington area of London. It seems that the junction of St Mark's Road and Cambridge Gardens had long been considered a dangerous corner, being 'blind' from both roads, and had caused numerous accidents. The decision by the local authorities to straighten out the nasty bend was influenced by the testimony of late-night motorists who claimed they had crashed at the junction while swerving to avoid a speeding double-decker bus that raced down St Mark's Road in the small hours, long after the normal buses had ceased service.

A typical report lodged with the Kensington police reads as follows: 'I was turning the corner and saw a bus tearing towards me. The lights of the top and bottom decks and the headlights were full on, but I could see no signs of either crew or passengers. I yanked my steering-wheel hard over and mounted the pavement, scraping the roadside wall. The bus just vanished!'

Following a fatal accident in which a driver swerved and hit the wall head-on, an eyewitness told the coroner's court that he had seen a mysterious bus hurtling down towards the car, just seconds before the driver spun off the road. When the coroner expressed cynicism, dozens of local residents wrote to his office, offering to testify that they too had seen the ghostly bus. Among the most impressive of these was a local transport official who claimed that he had seen the bus draw up at the bus depot in the early hours of the morning, stand with its engine running for a short while – and then disappear.

Shortly after the inquest, the wall which had claimed the driver's life was demolished under a road-widening scheme to make the junction safer. The eerie bus has never been seen since.

A ghostly tram haunts various stretches of Blackpool's famous tramway system, according to a number of reports. Several people claim to have heard it over the years, rattling along the promenade in the early hours of the morning. On one occasion, a tram inspector is said to have heard it approaching at about 6.30 on a dark morning. He looked round and saw a lighted tramcar approaching and held out his hand for it to stop – the tram never arrived.

Mrs Dugdale of Blackpool told me that one wet day she, her husband and their daughter were standing at the tram stop opposite the Claremont Hotel. She said: 'We heard a tram coming but there was nothing to be seen. The noise increased as the tram got closer, and as it passed, we all got our feet wet from the rain water thrown up from between the rails. Yet no visible tram passed us.' Mrs Dugdale went on to say that she and her husband have often heard the distinctive sound of a tram's air-horn as it leaves Manchester Square at around 2.30 in the morning. Yet, again, on investigation, there is never a tramcar to be seen.

In August 1931 an accident occurred on Garrowby Hill in the East Riding of Yorkshire, when a coach travelling from Bridlington to Liverpool collided with a car and crashed into a tree. Two of the passengers were killed and about twenty injured.

During the late autumn of that same year, rumours spread that this lonely road was haunted by a spectral vehicle which appeared out of the darkness travelling silently at enormous speed. It seemed to appear only on foggy or moonless nights, although the motorists who encountered it were in no doubt about its ghostly reality, rejecting forcibly the idea that it could have been a trick of the darkness. A series of accidents were attributed to the alarming passage of the phantom bus, and many locals were afraid to venture out at night for fear of meeting it. All the appearances of the spectral coach were made near the scene of the accident of the previous August, where at the roadside a five-foot cross was erected on a wooden base, in memory of the two people who had lost their lives.

A man who was driving to Bridlington one night said that he saw what appeared to be a huge vehicle silently approaching. Thinking it was a bus or lorry, he felt no fear. However, when the vehicle drew nearer he noticed that it made no sound but rushed towards him at great speed, causing him to take avoiding action. When he looked again, the mystery bus had disappeared and he had to concentrate hard to avoid going into the ditch.

*

During World War II, well over 1,000 tons of bombs were dropped on Liverpool. The Blitz of 1-8 May 1941 will live long in the memory and last in the history of the city. It was the worst week of sustained enemy raids on any part of Britain, an all-out attempt to wreck the port from which Western Approaches Command controlled the convoy system that fed the nation. The centre of the city lay waste, Huskisson No.2 Dock was obliterated when the SS *Malakand* blew up, and an ammunition train standing in Breckside siding was fired and exploded, devastating an entire district.

Among the thousands of people killed in Liverpool during that period was a well-respected and much-loved policeman who, when on his beat, would idly tap doors and railings with his truncheon as he passed. Whether this was as a warning to the local villains that he was approaching or just to let the old folks know he was around and it was safe, is not clear. During one of the raids in the May Blitz, oblivious of his own safety, he continued to patrol his beat, helping where necessary, pulling people to safety, offering advice or just reassuring the locals by his presence. Suddenly a bomb landed quite close to him as he patrolled the Lawrence Gardens area, one of the centre points of his beat, and he was blown to pieces.

In August 1971 residents of the area first saw the policeman's ghost. He was clearly visible strolling down the road, swinging his truncheon and tapping it gently against the house walls. One witness, not realizing he was seeing an apparition, was puzzled by the fact that he was wearing a haversack with a tin helmet strapped to it, and he tried to overtake him. On reaching the corner of the road, the apparition vanished, leaving the witness scratching his head in wonder.

Other hardy souls have attempted to catch up with him but, as they approached, he always disappeared as if into thin air.

One of the most remarkable modern ghost stories, which crops up all over the country, concerns a phantom hitch-hiker who, after being given a lift, vanishes while the car is still in motion. We have all heard the story of the driver who stops to pick up a pretty teenaged girl stranded at night at some remote country crossroads. He gives her the rear seat and, after a while, starts a conversation to which he receives no reply. Looking round, he finds the seat empty, apart from a handbag. Opening it, he finds the girl's address and, when he returns the handbag to her home, is shocked to learn that the girl had been killed at the very spot in the road where he picked her up. The fatal accident had occurred on that very night – a few years previously. Credulous nonsense?

Roy Fulton met the phantom hitch-hiker on a foggy Friday evening in October 1979. Stopping close to the small Bedfordshire village of Stanbridge on his way home from a darts match, the twenty-six-year-old carpet-fitter had no reason to suppose the figure at the roadside, thumb stuck up in the customary manner, was anything but human. True, the pale young man in the white shirt and dark trousers was uncommunicative, merely pointing towards Dunstable when asked where he wanted to go, but Mr Fulton knew from experience that some hitch-hikers are like that. It also crossed his mind that the stranger might be a deaf mute.

They had been travelling at a steady 40 mph for several minutes when Mr Fulton tried to break the ice by offering the hitch-hiker a cigarette. He turned to speak to him and was amazed that the man had disappeared. He stood on his brakes and had a quick look in the back to see if he had fallen off the seat or was ill, but there was no one there. Mr Fulton said: 'I just gripped the wheel and drove like hell!'

Despite the arguments for and against Mr Fulton's statement, he still insists that he gave a lift to a phantom hitch-hiker on that October night in 1979. Later he was interviewed by the police and by a journalist from the *Dunstable Gazette*, both of whom regard his testimony as reliable.

On 30 November 1974 Brian Mohan was driving his taxi-cab along the A6 back to Stockport, having just taken a fare to Whaley Bridge. Driving through Great Moor, he thought he caught a movement in his off-side driving-mirror reflecting the rear seat. Glancing into his rear-view mirror, he blinked with surprise, for he saw the reflection of an elderly woman sitting in the back seat. At the time he thought there must be some obvious explanation, a curious reflection or something of the kind, and he looked back to the road ahead and continued on past Stockport Convent.

As he approached the Davenport Theatre, Brian took a long look in the mirror. The figure of the woman was still there, sitting upright and quite motionless. There was nothing particularly striking about her, and even her expression conveyed nothing to the experienced driver, who began to feel very puzzled by the silent figure, for he knew he had not picked up a fare since leaving Whaley Bridge. Brian thought back over the past few hours. He'd had nothing to drink, he wasn't tired or in need of a rest, he wasn't hungry, and he had eaten nothing which would have given him hallucinations – yet there was a woman sitting impassively on the back seat of his cab whom he knew he had not stopped to pick up.

Just past Stockport Grammar School, he pulled into the side of the road and turned to open the glass partition and ask his mysterious passenger what she was up to. She had gone! He got out of his driving-seat, walked all round his cab and looked up and down the street. There was no sign of life and certainly no sign of the elderly woman who seconds before had been in his cab.

He later said: 'I saw her when we were in darkness, just as we passed the Convent, and I saw her when it was light, so it couldn't have been a reflected image. No one could have jumped into the cab, because the noise of the door, the movement on the springs and, of course, the courtesy light would have alerted me. I know I wasn't seeing things because I looked three times, just to make sure.' Brian described the woman in some detail. He said she was aged between about fifty and sixty and had long, thick hair. She wore a black overcoat with a pointed collar, a frilly white blouse and a black bow. He says he is quite sure he would recognize her again if he ever saw her – although he hopes he never does, for she cost him several restless nights afterwards.

For months after this, the black taxi-cab stood at the rear of the cab company's office in Lowfield Road. None of the drivers occupied in the private hire business would sit in it, let alone drive it!

In August 1970 the *Western Morning News* ran an interview with a Mrs K. Swithenbank, who said that, as she was driving from the village of Oake, along the A38, to her home in Taunton, Somerset, late one evening, she saw what she took to be a middle-aged man dressed in a long grey overcoat, standing in the centre of the road near the Hatherton Grange Hotel. His face was averted and he appeared to be carrying a torch, which he shone onto the roadway. As this was on a sharp bend, Mrs Swithenbank had no time to brake and she swerved violently. There was no impact, and when she looked back a moment later, the road was empty in both directions.

This short article brought a flood of reports. Two other motorists claimed that they had seen an identical figure in the same place and they had taken similar action. A motor-cyclist who encountered the figure some four miles to the west at White Ball fell from his motorbike and broke his leg, while another motorist said he had seen the figure at White Ball, but on this occasion the face was in clear profile, whereas on other occasions it had not been possible to make it out.

Then the *Exeter Express* published an amazing account by a Mr Harold Unsworth, a long-distance lorry-driver from Essex, who described how, at about three o'clock in the morning, he had been flagged down near the Blackbird Inn, about a mile from Hatherton Grange, by a middle-aged man in a grey overcoat and carrying a torch. It was a dark, wet and windy morning and the man, hatless and with curling grey hair hanging over his collar, seemed so wet and miserable that, despite the risk at such an hour on a lonely road, Mr Unsworth stopped to give him a lift.

Judging by the way he spoke, the stranger seemed to be well educated, and he asked to be dropped about four miles along the road at the old bridge at Holcombe. As they travelled, he delightedly described, with gruesome detail, the accidents that had happened along that stretch of road over the years. Mr Unsworth was not sorry to drop his strange passenger off.

Several days later, travelling along the A38 in the small hours, he was amazed when, reaching the same spot near the Blackbird Inn and in similar weather conditions, the same man flagged him down. Again he stopped to offer him a lift, and again the man asked to be dropped at the bridge.

A month later, the stranger was there again; the rain, the dark, the overcoat and even the conversation were the same. Mr Unsworth thought that perhaps the man was mentally ill, and he was relieved when, over the next few months, despite his passing the same spot several times, always in the early hours, the stranger was nowhere to be seen. However, in November he was there again and the same sequence of events followed – except that this time, when they stopped at the bridge, the man asked if the driver could wait until he collected some cases, as he wished to go further up the road.

Mr Unsworth waited for nearly half an hour in the pouring rain, and when the man didn't re-appear, he decided to drive on. But less than three miles ahead he saw someone frantically waving a torch to flag him down and as he approached he saw, with rising fear, the same figure in the grey overcoat and with the long, straggling grey hair. Yet it was not possible. No vehicle had passed him in either direction, and it was impossible that the man could have covered the distance from the bridge in so short a time on foot.

Thoroughly scared, he swerved to one side to pass the frantically waving figure. As he did so, the man leapt in front of the lorry at such a short distance that it was impossible to avoid hitting him. But there was no impact. Mr Unsworth braked hard, slightly jack-knifing the lorry, and came to rest a dozen yards away. Shaken, he climbed down from the cab and looked back. The figure was still standing in the centre of the road, shaking his fist and shouting obscenities at having been left behind. Then suddenly he was silent and, turning his back on the startled lorry-driver – he vanished.

His hair tingling, Mr Unsworth quickly climbed into his cab and drove furiously towards his destination. To this day, no one knows who this pathetic spectre is or why he seems doomed to seek a lift so desperately from passing vehicles.

One particular nasty I fervently hope I shall never meet cropped up regularly in conversation when I was researching a radio series in Cumbria recently. It is known as Bele Sheephead and to my knowledge has not been encountered since about 1972, when it caused havoc on the Broughton Moor road near Flimby, about halfway between Workington and Maryport.

Bele Sheephead is said to be half human, half sheep. According to tradition, when she was a young girl, Bele had a pet lamb which she allowed to wander unattended. One day, in her absence, the lamb was killed, its throat torn out by a fox. Despite her love for the animal, when Bele discovered it she felt no sorrow over its unfortunate demise, just an irresistible urge to drink the still warm blood which trickled from the open wound at its throat. Thus she acquired a taste for blood – in particular sheep's blood – and in time, so the legend goes, Bele became half sheep and gained her dubious nickname.

All this is legend, but there are many well-authenticated accounts of motorists coming to grief in the area after encountering something resembling the legendary Bele. The most consistent concerns a man and his wife, returning from Flimby by car, which ran out of petrol late at night. Telling his wife to remain in the car, the man went off in search of a garage and, during his long absence, probably due to the lateness of the hour, his wife fell into a light sleep.

She was sharply wakened by a noise which she realized, after a few seconds, was the klaxon of a police car rapidly approaching, followed by an ambulance. The police car pulled up sharply behind her own and a policeman approached, asking if she would mind stepping out of the vehicle but telling her not to look round. However, being a woman of a curious nature she did look round about her and was horrified to see her husband's decapitated body lying several yards away in the road. On top of a fence post on the bank beside the car was his severed head.

The case has never been solved. The unfortunate man was later buried in Flimby churchyard, where his grave can be found today. A victim, the locals believe, of Bele Sheephead.

Whilst in the Flimby area, keep an eye open for the spectre of 'Bible John', a figure dressed as a monk who carries a harmless-looking Bible. However, should one approach him too closely, he will open his hollowed-out Bible and remove from it a pistol, appearing as if to shoot the unfortunate victim. Thankfully, although there have been several recorded sightings over the years, to my knowledge no one has yet been killed by his gun.

One night early in the 1960s, two men travelling in a car along the A74 between Annan and Carlisle had what must qualify as the most terrifying experience of the century.

They had been touring the Borders in a small car and were on their way home after stopping off at Dumfries for a snack and some petrol. Just before midnight, they found themselves on the A74 with some twelve miles to go before reaching Carlisle. It was a dry, moonlit night, and the road stretched empty for several miles ahead of them.

Suddenly the car headlights picked up the figure of an old woman rushing towards them, waving her arms wildly. Before the driver had time to react, the figure simply vanished into thin air. But worse was to come, for the old woman then seemed to be followed by an endless stream of figures that loomed out of nowhere: cats, dogs, farm animals and an old man, long hair flying, who seemed to be screaming, yet no noise could be heard.

The driver kept swerving from side to side in an effort to miss colliding with the strange figures, until he suddenly realized that they had made no actual contact with the car. He therefore began to think it was his imagination. However, a quick glance at his passenger, sitting terrified and wild-eyed beside him, told him that this was no imagination: he was seeing the terrifying phantoms too.

As they continued to drive through the mass of open-mouthed and wild-looking creatures, there was a sudden drop in the temperature inside the vehicle, and the driver felt as if some force was trying to gain control of the car, wresting the steering-wheel from him. Both men began to feel suffocated, and on opening the window, bitter cold air rushed in, along with a cacophony of screaming, high-pitched laughter and cackling noises which seemed to be mocking the terrified occupants.

Unable to control the vehicle any longer, the driver pulled in at the roadside, and immediately they were attacked by an invisible and violent force which bombarded the car, rocking it from side to side until the two men began to feel sick. As one, they opened the doors and leapt out into the road – and immediately all went quiet. The road and countryside around were still and utterly deserted. Yet, as soon as they got back into the vehicle and shut the doors, the shaking and bouncing began again, this time accompanied by unearthly laughter. Invisible fists seemed to strike the car from every angle, and a high wind suddenly sprang up, adding to the terror.

Deciding that the only sensible thing to do was to get away from the place as quickly as possible, the driver pushed his passenger back into the car and, climbing in himself, re-started it and drove slowly through the weird figures which continued to loom suddenly out of nowhere and the terrifying noises which seemingly came from every direction. Often the figures would stop in the path of the car, as if daring the driver to run them down, but he drove a steady and straight course and, just as it seemed he would hit them, the strange figures evaporated.

After driving like this for about two miles, the two men suddenly saw ahead of them the comforting red glow of a vehicle's rear lights. As they drew nearer, they were relieved to find they were approaching a large furniture van. The driver suddenly became aware that the van was stationary and he was approaching it too fast. Exhausted by the previous events, his reactions were too slow and he discovered, to his horror, that there was no time to take evasive action; he was surely going to collide with the rear of the stationary vehicle.

Shouting a quick warning to his passenger, the driver steeled himself for the inevitable collision as the furniture van loomed larger and larger – and then, just before the moment of impact, it suddenly disappeared!

Shattered, drained of strength and totally mystified, the two men continued on their way, until they realized the car had slowed to a crawl. The noises and the high wind had died away and they were relieved to find themselves on the outskirts of Carlisle. The whole terrifying incident had lasted over thirty minutes.

No one knows what brought about the strange events of that night or who the ghostly figures were. There are tales that years ago witchcraft was practised in the area, but whether there was any connection one cannot be sure. And what about the phantom furniture van – what story lies behind that, one wonders?

Drive along the roads around Enfield in Middlesex, and you may encounter a well-authenticated phantom stage-coach. It has been seen on many occasions and to my knowledge was last seen as recently as the 1960s. It was seen and recorded in some detail in 1899 by three young women as they returned from their work at a factory at Ponders End.

In those days, the area behind the present Nags Head Road was open countryside, and the factory workers used a path through the fields to walk to and from work. The three girls said that the coach simply rose out of the ground, moved off in the direction of Brimsdown – and then disappeared. They said they clearly saw the figure of the driver and of someone leaning out of the window.

The *Enfield Gazette and Observer* took up the story around the turn of the century and gave more precise details of the phantom stage-coach after interviewing several witnesses. It heralded its approach with a shaft of light; it was drawn by two horses; it was all black, and the passengers were a man and two women wearing large hats; one of the women wears an emerald-green dress. The sounds of the horses' hooves and wheels can be heard quite distinctly – despite the fact that the animals and the vehicle appear to be moving at least eighteen inches above the ground.

Obstacles mean nothing to the phantom coachman. One report tells of the vehicle passing right through a house on the edge of the playing-fields belonging to Carterheath School and driving right through a room where a woman was sleeping. The reaction of the lady in question is not recorded. The coach usually appears well before midnight in the weeks leading up to Christmas, and the night is normally clear, cold and moonless.

The account of the sighting of the coach in the mid-1960s is quite vivid. A young man called Bob Byrd was cycling along Bell Lane to attend a meeting of the local Boys' Brigade when he saw two bright lights rushing towards him on his side of the road. Thinking a vehicle was approaching out of control, he began to dismount, but even before he had time to do so, the vehicle was on top of him. He said he saw two figures sitting between the lights and a third person behind them. The vague features ahead of the lights suggested horses. The vehicle came rushing towards him, a few feet off the ground, and only as the apparition passed right through him did he get an impression of a jet-black, four-wheeled vehicle.

The Enfield stage-coach remains a mystery, for no local record provides a solution. The only theory is that the road on which the phantom is seen is an ancient one, which formerly ended beside the River Lea. Locals believe that some private coach may have come to grief by being driven into the river on a winter's night, sometime back in the eighteenth century.

8. Ghosts Without Reason

Ghosts, as innumerable studies have shown, are a world-wide phenomenon which have been recorded throughout history, appearing in a variety of shapes and forms and without seeming, in many cases, to have or serve any purpose. The most widespread is, of course, the ghost of a human being, appearing sometimes as solid-looking as one's neighbour or as a mist-like entity, roughly human in shape and disappearing as mysteriously and as suddenly as it appeared. Yet, despite investigation by experts, the Church and other institutions and societies interested in paranormal phenomena, many of the reported sightings remain a complete mystery, and any explanation as to the reasoning behind them is, at the most, inspired guesswork.

Mrs C.J. Malpas of Chorley, Lancashire, is under no kind of delusion about the ghost which frequented the house she and her family lived in some years ago.

She told me that the ghost was with them all the time they lived in the house, a mysterious but friendly shade who did no harm to anyone, although she did have an annoying habit of opening and shutting doors. She said: 'We lived in the house about forty years, and my father-in-law lived there before us and had experienced the ghost himself. We nicknamed it "Aunt Emma". None of my husband's sisters would go to the bathroom, always preferring to use the outside toilet.'

Mrs Malpas' son, who was about six years old at the time of this incident, suffered very badly from asthma. One night he called out from his bedroom that a lady with long black hair was standing at the foot of his bed. 'I told him it was an angel and that she was watching over him,' she said. 'He believed me and fell asleep again.'

This occurred several times, until one day Mrs Malpas confronted the figure herself, one Saturday afternoon in broad daylight. She continued: 'She was standing on the landing at the top of the stairs. I said to her "Who are you?", at which she suddenly disappeared!'

On another occasion the mysterious figure was seen to come out of one of the bedrooms and walk downstairs. Every stair creaked as she passed over it – yet when any member of the family went up or down there was never a creak from them. 'The dog was going frantic, and her fur stood up along the full length of her back,' said Mrs Malpas. 'Then the ghost appeared in the bedroom where my second son slept. A woman with black hair, who just stood at the foot of the bed.'

No amount of research by the family has brought forth any explanation as to why the phantom haunted the house for all those years, and they never did discover her identity.

The seventeenth-century schoolhouse at Reagill in Cumbria has no particularly untoward history, and there is no explanation for its haunting.

In November 1959 a young couple moved into the house and not long afterwards saw the ghost of a woman, in old-fashioned dress. It was about five o'clock in the morning, and the husband was lying awake, when suddenly the figure of a woman materialized between the window and the dressing-table. He felt a prickly feeling, as the hair rose at the back of his neck, when the figure walked round the bed and paused, gazing at the wall against which the bed stood. The figure then turned and walked to a point opposite the foot of the bed, where it stood for a few seconds before it suddenly vanished.

The figure was in view for a full half minute. The face was indistinct, but he could see it was a woman by her dress and hairstyle. At first he thought he must have been dreaming or that it was a figment of his imagination, but then his wife suddenly remarked, 'This place is haunted!' She went on to describe to him what she had seen, which, without any prompting by him, was a description of the ghostly incident exactly as he had witnessed it. She confirmed that the figure was that of a woman wearing a high, stiff-necked blouse, with her hair piled up on her head.

She also admitted that on another occasion, when her husband had been asleep, she had seen the figure in approximately the same place, although for a shorter period. To date there has been no satisfactory explanation of this phenomenon, and I understand that it is some time since the ghostly female has been seen.

Mr Albert Paradise has lived in Stainland, near Halifax in Yorkshire, for over sixty years and until a few years ago he had lived with his father, until his death, in a cottage a few hundred yards down the road.

Mr Paradise told me: 'The building was erected in 1705. We moved in about 1920. My father had a fear of gas and electricity, considering them to be highly dangerous, and so from 1920 up until his death in the 1950s we survived on nothing more than a coal fire for cooking on and oil lamps and candles for lighting.' In the thirty-five years that he and his father had lived in the cottage, they had never seen or heard anything, but following the old man's death a number of mysterious events took place, culminating in one incident which, Mr Paradise said, 'frightened the life out of me'.

It was New Year's Eve 1956. Because he didn't have any electricity in the house, he used to go to bed reasonably early and listen to an old accumulator-operated radio set. He does not drink, so he could not be accused of having been celebrating the New Year. He said: 'Because it was a moonlit night, I left the bedroom curtains open and lay in bed fully awake, listening to some classical music on the old Third Programme. The bed was facing the fireplace, and over the mantelpiece was an old Victorian framed print. Suddenly a face seemed to appear in the frame in place of the picture and then, to my absolute terror, a figure appeared, as if walking out of the fireplace from the house next door, which floated towards the bottom of the bed. His face was a ghastly white and he had sunken eyes and long, flowing hair, which was as white as his face.'

The figure appeared to be playing a violin, his head moving from side to side, long hair shaking as if in time to the radio. Mr Paradise admits to having raced from the bedroom in sheer terror.

A couple of nights later he was making his supper in the kitchen when he got the feeling that someone was standing behind him. Too afraid to turn around, he shouted, 'Oh, not tonight! Go away, please!' He said that he sat in the kitchen for the whole night, too afraid to go to bed. There does not appear to be any record of other incidents in the house prior to these, and I am told that, once the fireplace had been bricked up and electricity installed, there were no further incidents.

The ghostly experience of Mrs Violet Nicholls of Wolverhampton began, like most hauntings, in a straightforward manner, but it was to develop into something out of the ordinary.

One night in 1952 thirty-four-year-old Mrs Nicholls woke up and saw a young woman in her mid-twenties standing in the bedroom. She appeared to be an attractive young woman with a flawless skin, long blonde hair and a full-length yellow dress. Thoroughly scared, Mrs Nicholls woke her husband, who reluctantly got up and searched the house for intruders. Finding nothing, he went back to bed, quite annoyed, and was soon fast asleep again. Mrs Nicholls was too shaken to go back to sleep. She knew what she had seen and knew it was not imagination. Lying awake in the darkened room, she saw the bedroom door open and the same young woman put her head round the door, looked around as if checking that everything was in order – and simply vanished!

Around midday, some six or seven days later, Mrs Nicholls was alone in the house when she happened to glance out of the window and saw the same young woman, her hair swinging, walking up the path towards the house. Surprised, Mrs Nicholls watched as the figure passed the kitchen door and again vanished. Nothing more was seen of the mysterious apparition, and the incident would probably have been forgotten had it not been for something which occurred some six years later.

By then, Mrs Nicholls was living alone and bringing up her five-year-old son. One evening she sent him up to bed, to undress, then followed him up some minutes later to tuck him in. But he wasn't undressed, he was staring in bewilderment at the floor near the bedroom fireplace. The boy pointed excitedly to a large knot-hole in the floorboards. Mrs Nicholls looked and, almost too taken aback to believe what she saw, stared open-mouthed as a pale blue, unmistakably human eye, stared back at her from the shallow void between the floorboards and the downstairs ceiling.

She and her son stood shaking with fear as the eye, which at first appeared frightened – then watchful – stared unblinking upwards, moving from time to time up and down, as if trying to escape. Finally it seemed to drift slowly to one side and, although it did not disappear for a further ten minutes or so, it eventually melted away.

The strange incident was never repeated and no one has been able to come up with an explanation for the frightening events of that evening in 1958.

A rather mundane but unusual haunting took place in Brighton, Sussex, in 1910, at Whitechurch House, a large detached residence facing Preston Park on the main road into the town. Whitechurch House stood in its own grounds, having its own stables and coachhouse. Inside the house, leading off from the dining-room, was a small room, known to the family as 'the den', which had french windows opening onto the lawn.

One of the maids at Whitechurch House at that time was Mrs M. Holland, whose job it was each morning at six-thirty to clean the 'den'. She said: 'At exactly this time each morning the french windows would slowly open and then slowly close again, as if someone was trying to creep into the house unnoticed. At first I assumed it was the wind, or that one of the other maids was playing tricks on me, but then I discovered that there was no wind, nor were there any other servants about in that part of the house.'

What was particularly strange was that, when the doors opened, they were, in fact, securely locked and bolted – and so they were *after* they had closed again!

This occurred nearly every morning just after 6.30 and the puzzled Mrs Holland, try as she might, could find no logical explanation for it. She attempted to stop the french windows while they were slowly opening, but she found it was impossible, for they were being opened by some strong, irresistible force. On one occasion she pre-empted the phenomenon by opening the french windows before six-thirty – and they immediately slammed shut and waited until it was the proper time! On each occasion the doors opened in this way, cold air would envelop the 'den' regardless of the weather outside or the time of year.

Becoming rather frightened, Mrs Holland told the master of the house. At first he dismissed the whole thing with Edwardian fervour as 'stuff and nonsense', but one morning, when he himself was up early to go to London, he witnessed the phenomenon for himself and was visibly shaken by the experience.

In fact, it was not long afterwards that he sold up and Mrs Holland had to find other employment. The house was left empty for some time, due to the family's rather hurried departure, and the mystery of the french windows was never solved.

Tony Atkins paid next to nothing for his gas supply for twelve years thanks to a ghost – and he has the gas bills to prove it.

His unusual experience began in 1970 after he had moved into his new home in Watford, Hertfordshire, with his wife and two daughters. Tony, a fifty-year-old electronics inspector, said: 'One night we heard crying in the hall. There was no one there when I went to look, but the area under the stairs, where the gas meter was, was ice-cold.' He said he thought someone was playing a practical joke, but the same thing happened again the following night and kept on happening.

'One night,' said Tony, 'my wife said a woman's hand had brushed hers, so I stuck my head in the cupboard under the stairs and shouted, "If there's a ghost in this house, show me." ' To his amazement, the dial on the gas meter stopped recording. He said: 'We turned on every gas appliance in the house. The meter should have been fairly whizzing round – but it stayed still.' It stayed like that for a long time, either moving very slowly or stopped completely. The local Gas Board engineers could find nothing wrong, despite the fact that the gas bills were a ridiculous £10 a quarter.

'Sometimes,' Tony continued, 'we would see the shadowy shape of a woman in a long dress, although now we have got quite used to her.' In time, neighbours suggested this could possibly be the ghost of a young Polish woman who had committed suicide in the cupboard under the stairs during the Second World War. Her description fitted that of the shadowy figure seen by the Atkins family.

Tony concluded: 'When they told me that, I stuck my head in the cupboard and said, "Rest in peace. God go with you", and the cold spot simply went, the meter began working properly and we started getting normal gas bills.' He said the ghost is still around, although he feels sure she is now at peace. There is now no crying, no cold spots, no odd goings-on – and no explanation as to why she should suddenly begin to haunt the house.

Most people can't wait to finish school, but a ghost nicknamed 'Horace' just won't leave. He is thought to be the spirit of a former caretaker of St George's Primary School in Hull and seems to be keeping an eye on the present caretaker, Steve Norris, who, along with the school cleaners, has seen him several times.

Steve says Horace is a friendly enough spectre and he has got used to seeing him around, though sometimes the ghost feels like throwing an exercise book at him. Other times he goes a bit too far with his tricks, switching lights off and on and sometimes putting all the chairs down, after the children have put them up on the desks. The figure wears a long blue warehouse coat and is said to be about five feet nine inches tall, although no one has been able to get a really clear look at him.

Steve Norris first realized that something was wrong when he was alone in the school one evening and caught sight of a figure going past a classroom he was cleaning. He said: 'I saw this figure heading towards part of the school which I knew was locked. I thought to myself, "He'll have to come back this way", because there was no way he could go through the locked door and I was the only one with the keys.'

The figure did not return, nor could Steve find any trace of him. Next morning he mentioned it to the cleaners, who replied cheerfully, 'Oh, that's just Horace – our ghost!' Then Steve asked the headmaster about it and was told that many years ago a caretaker had collapsed and died in the school cellar. Now everyone assumed that Horace was his ghost.

An inexplicable and intriguing mystery surrounds Craster Tower, just off the B1399 road at Alnwick in Northumberland. This tower, which was built about 1290, with a more recent eighteenth-century addition, is about seventy feet high and forty feet square and originally contained just three rooms. The incident which occurred there a few years ago has left more than one member of the household puzzled.

One morning, before breakfast, the maid asked the owner if he would go with her to the dining-room before she touched anything. On entering, he discovered that the place was in a shambles. On either side of the mantelpiece there stood two large, heavy Chinese vases. One had been completely broken in half, with the upper part lying horizontally where it had stood, while the other half lay unbroken in the fender. Just behind the firescreen lay a pile of soot.

But the strangest thing was that a window seat, some five yards away, had been unaffected by the fall of soot, and yet there was a perfect sooty outline of a naked human foot – just one foot – on the otherwise untouched window seat.

This was not the only incident which occurred at Craster Tower. Other mysterious goings-on include strange bangs and thumps, which appear to emanate from the wall which divides the front and back libraries. But the best-known and most-reported phantom is that of an unknown 'grey lady', a mysterious spectre who has been witnessed by dozens of people over the past few years.

In August 1955 she was reported by a young girl who saw the figure open the front door and drift upstairs to the drawing-room. If she is not seen, her presence is notified by the sound of her skirts rustling as she passes, drifting from the first-floor front landing window and moving slowly towards the pele tower, where she vanishes.

In quite recent years the sound of a coach and horses has been heard, coming to a stop at the front door. Although the night was clear and the drive was lit by a brilliant moon, when the occupants rushed to open the door, nothing could be seen. Then, after a few minutes, the phantom carriage was heard to move off again and drive towards the stables, round the back of the building.

Just who the grey lady is, where the coach comes from or what they both represent, no one has so far been able to discover.

In a small, neat house at Ushaw Moor, just off the B6802, not far from the centre of Durham, Ben Chicken lived in dread of the return of a ghost that had haunted him for nearly forty years – a ghost which came to be known as 'the Silent Summoner'.

The story began in 1937, when a man called John Mahon died, leaving a young widow, Jane, and five children. At that time the Depression had bitten deep into the north-east of England, so, to make ends meet, Mrs Mahon took in a lodger, twenty-seven-year-old Ben Chicken. In a very short time, Ben and Jane fell in love and in 1938 they married. Then came the Second World War, and in 1942 Jane's second son by her former husband, Robert Mahon, joined the armed forces.

One night in 1944, Ben Chicken woke up to find the figure of a man in working clothes standing silently beside the bed, staring hard at him. After several minutes the figure vanished, but the incident made such a deep impression on him that at breakfast Ben poured out his experience and gave a description of every detail of the figure, its face and the way it was dressed.

He failed to notice the look of fear which came over his wife's face, until she stammered out that he had given an incredibly accurate description of her first husband – a man Ben had never seen. Ben went off to work puzzled and not a little apprehensive. This apprehension was tragically justified, for later in the day a telegram arrived informing Jane that young Robert had been killed in action.

For the next six months the apparition appeared with alarming regularity, bringing with it more apprehension, but gradually the appearances became less frequent, until they ceased altogether.

The war came to an end, the remaining four children married and life began to improve for Ben and Jane Chicken. They were able to forget about the sinister spectre of John Mahon and begin to move gently towards a contented middle age.

Then, in 1973, the visitations began again, after a period of thirty years. The ghost of John Mahon was back, for what purpose Ben didn't know. It stood beside the bed, silent and ominous, and for several weeks afterwards Ben prayed in vain that come bedtime the menacing figure would not re-appear. But it continued to appear, and Ben knew in his heart of hearts that it was the omen of some forthcoming disaster.

When it came, it wasn't altogether unexpected. Returning home from work one day, Ben found his wife collapsed on the floor. She'd had a stroke and, after she had lingered speechless for nearly three weeks, the 'Silent Summoner's' purpose became all too obvious. Jane Chicken died on 3 August 1973, aged seventy-one. Now, without his beloved Jane, Ben lived an empty life. Even the sinister figure had disappeared, its purpose apparently accomplished. Time could not heal and so the shock was as keen as ever when, in the autumn of 1975, Ben woke to find the sinister apparition at his bedside once more.

This time, instead of fear, Ben felt only anger. Why had this ominous form returned? What more could it want from him? The poor chap did not have long to wait to find out.

The very next day he received news that Jane's youngest son, Vincent Mahon, had collapsed over the wheel of his lorry and had later died in hospital. From then on, Ben Chicken lived in dread of the recurring phantom. The next time the 'Silent Summoner' appeared, there was only one other person he could come for – Ben Chicken!

In January 1974 Geoffrey White, from Colchester, and three friends travelled to Manchester to watch their football team, Ipswich Town, play Manchester United.

At about 11 a.m. they made a stop at the Keele Service Station on the M6 Motorway, where Geoffrey and one of his mates hurried to the lavatory, leaving their two companions in the car. There were only a few people in the lavatory at the time, but the man standing at the urinal between Geoffrey and his friend riveted their attention.

Geoffrey told local newspapers: 'He was like one of those pictures you see of Puritans. He wore a wide-brimmed hat, a broad white collar and roughly woven light brown clothes. One thing I particularly noticed was the coarse stitching.' When the man left, they wondered who he could be and decided he was probably connected with some advertising stunt. Mildly intrigued, they hurried after him, only to find once they got outside that there was not a trace of the man to be seen.

They asked their two companions, who had remained in the car, but they were adamant that no such person had come out of the lavatory. They would surely have noticed someone dressed as strangely as that. This only added to the mystery, for there seemed nowhere he could possibly have gone. However, the four young men carried on to the match and in the excitement of the game the mysterious man in Puritan clothes was forgotten.

Some months later, Geoffrey was standing at the window of his home, which faces the Siege House in Colchester. This is a bullet-pitted building which was one of the last strongholds of the supporters of King Charles I before they surrendered to Cromwell's troops. Suddenly he gave a shout – the very same figure he had seen at the Keele Service Area was walking slowly along the pavement opposite!

The odd thing about it was that no one in the busy street seemed to be taking any notice of the strangely dressed figure. Geoffrey's frantic yell brought his wife and his mother-in-law dashing into the room. His wife said that all she could see were ordinary people in ordinary clothes passing by. But his mother-in-law stood absolutely astounded, as she described in detail the figure Geoffrey had first seen at a Service Area in Staffordshire some hundred miles away.

To this day, the mystery has never been explained.

Weird sounds, footsteps on the stairs, moving furniture and ghostly apparitions: these are the ingredients of every good ghost story – and all these things happened in a cottage in the village of Longnor, which stands on the borders of Staffordshire, not far from the town of Leek. The disturbances became so violent that the occupant was forced to leave after the hauntings became known not only nationally but internationally, thanks to media attention.

Following the death of his mother in 1959, Mr Wood lived alone at the cottage. Just before Christmas 1960, he had come out of hospital following an operation, and it was some considerable time before he was able to return to work. The first unusual occurrence took place in late January 1961, when Mr Wood went to bed around ten o'clock at night and was wakened a couple of hours later by someone, or something, in his bedroom. Then, still half asleep, he felt an ice-cold hand firmly grip his own. Believing it was his imagination, Mr Wood thought little about it at the time.

A few nights later, again during the small hours, he was wakened by a loud noise. It sounded as if someone had dropped a galvanized bucket on the kitchen floor. Again he thought he must have been dreaming, and he certainly never gave a thought to the possibility of ghosts. However, what followed in the next few days was to change his mind.

The following night, he was just going to bed and had reached the top of the stairs when there was a terrific crash which sounded as if the ceiling in one of the bedrooms had fallen in. The sound of falling plaster lasted some time. Unnerved, he did not look into that bedroom until the following day, but when he did, he discovered that nothing had been disturbed. There was no fallen ceiling, no beam or plaster. Everything was as it should be.

For several weeks after that, nothing else happened. Then one day, as he was sitting quietly reading the newspaper, there was another terrific crash as numerous cardboard cartons came bumping down the stairs. He knew there was no one else in the cottage at the time – and where had the cartons come from?

Soon afterwards, Mr Wood saw something which gave him a terrible fright. He was lying in bed, wide awake, when he saw the latch of his bedroom door lift silently. The door opened a few inches and then stopped, as though being held by some unseen hand. Then, slowly, it began to open wider, and there, framed in the doorway, stood the figure of an old woman. She was wearing a black dress and a black cape, and she had silver white hair. The strange woman walked towards the bed and then moved to one side, before appearing to walk right through a large, old-fashioned wardrobe. Mr Wood sat up in bed paralysed with fear. After this, he said, he always slept with the bedroom light on.

But even more frightening than the strange figure were the mysterious sounds which filled the house almost daily. Every morning, between six and seven o'clock, a noise could be heard downstairs which sounded as though someone was unrolling lengths of wallpaper and then cutting it. Lights began to click on and off, the living-room light would go off and the kitchen light would be switched on. Footsteps could be heard frequently around the house, accompanied by a strange whistling. When these footsteps were heard on the stairs, they were heavy, sounding like those of a man clomping up in heavy boots.

Crockery, pans and other utensils were thrown about. Pans would be knocked off shelves with a terrific clatter. The low growl of a dog was often heard coming from the hearth in front of the fireplace – yet no dog was ever seen. Knocks at the front door were another frequent annoyance, for whenever Mr Wood went to answer the door, there was never anyone there.

On another occasion, Mr Wood's cousin had her cardigan torn off her back. Bedclothes were thrown violently to the floor; curtains would be torn down from the windows, often followed by a gust of cold air, despite the fact that the windows were firmly closed and fastened.

Eventually Mr Wood was forced to leave the cottage that had been his home for many years. He felt the place was not only haunted but had taken on utterly evil characteristics. It was as though the spirits – or whatever they were – were trying to drive him out. They certainly succeeded. Mr Wood went to live in Leek, some seven miles away.

Today no one knows who or what haunted the cottage, or even if it is still haunted. Nor does anyone know why the hauntings should have begun so suddenly. The cottage remained empty for some time after Mr Wood left, and I am told that there was talk of its being demolished.

In 1947 two middle-aged spinsters holidaying in Perranporth, Cornwall, became the focus of a haunting which has intrigued and bewildered for forty years.

They arrived at the holiday village late in the afternoon and were extremely annoyed to discover that, instead of the new mobile home they had been promised, they were allocated an old chalet – more like a dilapidated wooden shack, consisting of nothing more than a tiny living-room, a bedroom and what was laughingly called 'the kitchen'. It was in the early season and many of the chalets and caravans were unoccupied, so they felt that the site-owner had treated them rather shabbily. But, tired after a long train journey, they settled in and, after a wash and unpacking, had a light meal and went to bed early.

About 11.30 p.m. they were disturbed by the sound of stealthy footsteps padding around outside their chalet, and of a dog growling at the door. Nervously, both women peered out of the bedroom window, but as it was a dark, moonless night, they could see nothing. Hoping that the flimsy walls would provide some form of protective barrier, they settled down again, feeling a little uneasy.

After a short time they heard the unmistakable sound of the chalet door opening and being slammed shut again. This frightened the two women, who knew that it had been securely locked and bolted most carefully. Then they became aware of padding footsteps prowling round the living-room. Terrified, one of the women called out, 'Who's there?' It was followed by a heavy, ominous silence, making both women think, for a time at least, that the stranger had taken fright and had left – or else he was waiting silently in the darkened room, ready to pounce!

Some minutes later, they were amazed to hear the rustling of paper, as if someone was turning over the pages of a newspaper. This was followed by a jolly, gentle chuckle devoid of any malice or evil. It was as if someone had entered the living-room and was enjoying reading something amusing in the daily paper. The rustling of the paper came again as whoever it was turned another page, followed by laughter and an unidentifiable creaking noise.

Taking a deep breath, the two women bravely got out of bed and, arming themselves with whatever objects they could lay their hands on, decided to tackle the intruder at the other side of the bedroom wall.

As they threw open the door, the whole of the small living-room was visible – and there was no one there. Nor was there any place where anyone could have hidden. But, scalps tingling, they saw immediately that the wicker rocking-chair was swaying backwards and forwards with eerie regularity. It was not the swaying one experiences when someone gets out of the chair and it is left to run down; this was the steady and equal rocking of a chair being rocked backwards and forwards by some invisible person seated in it.

Again, from the chair there came the eerie but cheery

laugh and the crackling of the newspaper. Then, as the women nervously drew nearer, a low warning snarl of an unseen dog, which seemed to be located by the side of the rocking-chair, made them stop dead in their tracks. Once more there came the phantom chuckling accompanied by a more insistent growl from the invisible dog.

. At this point the women's nerve broke. They fled back into the bedroom, barricaded the door and sat huddled together with the light on until daybreak, their nerves taut and strained. From time to time they heard the footsteps padding around the living-room and occasionally the jolly chuckle. As soon as the sun rose, they packed their cases and sat on the beach until the rest of the camp began to wake; then they went to find the site owner.

The site owner listened carefully to their story and, to their surprise, said that she had been told about this by other visitors in the past. Apologizing profusely, she offered the women one of her latest luxury caravans for the remainder of their holiday, where the days and nights passed uneventfully.

Today the old chalet has been long gone, and it has not even been possible to discover exactly where it stood, to discover the identity of the chuckling ghost, which remains as much a mystery today as it did forty years ago.

And finally, just when you thought it was safe to go to sleep, let us examine a haunted seaside boarding-house, just one of several to be found in the Las Vegas of the North – Blackpool.

If there are ghosts in that lively resort – and more psychic researchers visit Blackpool every year – surely they would not hover around the gale-lashed promenade or the deserted rain-swept beaches? No, they will be found behind the net curtains of the bland boarding-houses where who-knows-what secret tragedies have been enacted.

The Rigby family, John, Mary and their young son, Martin, had been looking forward to their two weeks holiday in Blackpool for months. But this year was going to be a little different. They were unable to lodge at the boarding-house they had stayed at in previous years, but the new one they found was pleasant, the food homely but good and the bedroom comfortable. Then, on their third night, things began to go terribly wrong.

Mary Rigby had gone to bed before her husband, who had gone for a late-night stroll along the promenade. Martin was fast asleep in the small bed in the corner. Within minutes of turning out the light, Mrs Rigby sensed a change in the atmosphere of the room. Lying there, tired but not quite able to sleep, she found her eyes continually straying towards the deep, oval mirror set in the front of the big old wardrobe.

She was just drifting off to sleep when she saw it – a swirling, misty blue shape forming in the mirror. It seemed to ooze out of the mirror towards her, and she distinctly felt the pressure of ice-cold fingers on her throat. Fortunately, at that moment, the door opened and in walked her husband.

Two nights later it was John Rigby's turn. His startled wife was wakened by a dreadful gurgling noise coming from him. When she shook him awake, he told her that he must have been having some sort of a nightmare. He said he felt as if someone was trying to strangle him. However, when, two nights after that, young Martin came screaming to his parents, shouting that a man had come out of the mirror and had tried to choke him, John and Mary Rigby finally admitted to themselves that there was something very, very wrong about their room. Despite the fact that their holiday was only half over, the Rigbys packed their belongings and went back home.

The boarding-house in question can still be found in the town, and it still takes in visitors during the summer season. Whether other people have experienced the same uncanny sensations as the Rigbys, I have been unable to discover. Who or what haunts the place I have no idea – except that there may be some connection between the house and the 'brides-in-the-bath' killer, George Joseph Smith. But he drowned his victims; he didn't strangle them!

9. Unbidden Guests

Many of the inns of England are reputed to be haunted; just how many of them actually are is open to conjecture. However, it must be remembered that a number of old inns go back a long way in history and were the focal point of community life, especially that of a village. It is not surprising, then, that tales of haunted beer cellars, footsteps along dimly lit passages, faces at windows and suchlike have been handed down from generation to generation.

Country inns are more suited to such tales, of course, and many have a room or rooms in which the wraith of a former landlord or guest is supposed to appear from time to time. The country pub, set back from the lonely road, deep in the heart of some bleak moorland spot, with its wooden sign swinging in the wind and its rusty hinges issuing ghostly creaks, creates just the right atmosphere for a haunting, be it fact or fiction.

There are so many allegedly haunted pubs and inns in the country that the main problem in writing about them is in deciding which ones to leave out. Those in this chapter have been selected at random from some of the thousands which are said to be haunted in England alone.

The Town of Ramsgate, an old pub in Wapping, stands by the River Thames and is said to be haunted by the ghost of the infamous 'hanging judge', Lord Chief Justice George Jeffries, who presided over the Bloody Assizes of 1685, when hundreds of people implicated in the Monmouth Rebellion were either executed or sent into slavery in the Colonies.

155

The fairly modern frontage of the pub dates only from the 1930s, but the main fabric of the building and the Wapping Stairs leading from the back of the pub to the river are over 300 years old. It was on these stairs that Judge Jeffries was himself arrested in 1688, when he tried to flee the country disguised as a sea-farer. He was taken to the Tower of London, where he died before he could come to trial. The panic he felt on his arrest appears to have imprinted itself on the old pub, and his ghost has haunted it ever since his death, although it does appear to have altered somewhat over the years.

Some people have identified the ghost with its grim features from contemporary portraits, while others have reported seeing a Cavalier in a periwig and velvet breeches or as a grey-haired man in a long nightshirt. Nevertheless, so many sightings have been reported over the years by so many different witnesses, including the Thames river police, that the spectre of this old tavern surely deserves to be rated as genuine.

The Chequers Inn on London Road in Amersham, Buckinghamshire, was built in the fifteenth century and, apart from acquiring modern lighting and heating arrangements etc, has changed very little since.

Numerous landlords have apparently come and gone in quick succession after being disturbed by moaning sounds and the occasional sighting of a white hooded figure floating silently through one of the bedrooms. One day in 1971 a barman described to the licensee the figure of a man wearing a long cloak, who appeared to be trying to climb up the bar chimney. The licensee could see nothing but, in discussing the barman's description of what he claimed to have seen with some of the regulars, he was assured that this was the ghost of old Osman, who had been seen many times over the years.

Weird shrieking screams have echoed through the low-beamed corridors and passages late at night, yet nothing can be found to account for them. Doors have been found open which should have been closed, and the young daughter of a former landlord was frightened by the robed figure which walked around the dressing-table in her bedroom, before disappearing through a locked door.

It appears that shortly after the inn was opened, some 400 years ago, a group of religious martyrs spent their last night on this earth chained to a beam inside the inn, under the guard of a local warder called Osman. The following morning they were burned at the stake a few hundred yards away, at a place called Rectory Woods. Osman later died in complete misery, only in his early thirties, and it is thought to be his grieving spirit which has returned to roam the stairways and passages.

The St Anne's Castle an old inn at Great Leighs in Essex, claims to be the oldest inn in England and for as long as anyone can remember it has been famous for its haunted room. There are well over a hundred signed statements from people who have attempted to spend a night there at different times and who have had curious experiences to relate.

One visitor attempting to sleep in the haunted room was suddenly wakened by loud cries. He jumped quickly out of bed and the noises ceased, only to re-commence when he lay down again. This continued time after time, and he had no rest until daybreak. Not long afterwards a girl occupied the room for one night and spent most of the time huddled by the window waiting for the dawn. Several people have reported seeing a black shape in the room, usually on one particular side of the bed.

Noises of various kinds have been reported: thuds, shuffles, bangs and raps, seemingly coming from the direction of the door, and the sound of furniture moving around; a cold draught has been felt and curtains have been torn down; bed-clothes have been ripped off beds and clothing scattered about the room.

There are various stories which attempt to explain the manifestations. One of the most persistent concerns the alleged murder of a child in the four-poster bed which once filled this room. The child was said to have been murdered in the presence of its mother, many years ago.

Whether this is the cause, or whether it is due to the fact that the inn has also been the retreat of monks, Royalists and highwaymen, no one really knows.

Still in Essex, the Golden Fleece, another ancient inn in Brentwood, is reputed to stand on the site of the twelfth-century St Peter's Priory. The main hall and wings are fifteenth-century, with later additions. One interesting aspect, as far as the visitor is concerned, is a room where Lord Nelson is said to have stayed when he was *en route* for Harwich, and it is carefully preserved just as he left it. The pub was certainly used as a staging-post on the London-Harwich run, and one of the traditions associated with it was that the old waggoners would pay the landlord a halfpenny to warm their food in the big ovens, while they attended to their horses.

Some years ago a lady saw a ghost in the pub, and her granddaughter also saw the apparition of a monk. One lady guest, while in one of the upstairs rooms, saw the figure of a monk with his arms folded, reflected in a mirror and staring intently at her. When she turned to face him, the monk had vanished. She returned to her former position only to find him still watching her in the glass! Other phenomena have been experienced for a number of years, such as pots, pans and glasses being inexplicably moved around in the kitchen and in the bar.

Many visitors to Penzance in Cornwall will have sampled the beverages provided by mine host at The Dolphin Inn, the ancient waterside pub which was the headquarters of Sir John Hawkins when he was enlisting Cornishmen to fight the Spanish Armada in 1588. Judge Jeffries is reputed to have held his court there in what is today the dining-room, the prisoners being kept in the cellars, where the old kitchen range and lavatory can still be seen today. During repairs a few years ago, proof was found – if proof was needed – that the inn had been used by smugglers, for in the old days Penzance was the first call for ships homeward bound from the Americas, and it is said that the Dolphin was where the first potatoes were eaten and where the first tobacco was ever smoked in England. While a bedroom was being redecorated a few years ago, a door was discovered which led to a small secret closet in the roof, so this too is thought to have been used by smugglers, to hide either themselves or their loot from the revenue men.

This really is an interesting old inn, full of character, made all the more interesting by the fact that it is haunted by an old sea-captain in a tricorn hat and laced ruffles. Although his footsteps have been heard as recently as 1985, the captain's ghost has not been seen for some years now. I was told that several people have heard heavy, measured footsteps crossing the room above the bar, which pass towards the rear of the building. The footsteps never return, suggesting that perhaps the old sea-dog whoever he was, took a journey from which he too never returned.

Another haunted Cornish pub is the Manor House Inn at Rilla Mill, just off the B3275 Plymouth road. This inn, well off the beaten track, is on a narrow road which leads to romantic Bodmin Moor, and it was here, in the 1960s, that the licensee reported having heard phantom footsteps for many years, in an upstairs room which has always been empty. Many of the regulars have heard the noises and accept them as part of the character of the place, although they are not always so happy about the inexplicable ice-cold draught that often sweeps through.

Sceptics have said that this is caused by atmospheric pressure, which in turn is caused by the closeness of the River Linner. Atmospheric pressure or not, this does not account for the mysterious heavy footsteps walking across the floor of an empty room.

Across the border in Devon, the Old Smugglers Inn at Coombe Cellars, near Teignmouth, is another very old inn. It was at one time known as the Ferryboat and was frequented by lightermen taking loads of Dartmoor stone to London for the building of the 'new London Bridge' – now domiciled in the USA. Earlier than this, it was a rendezvous point for Lord Nelson, who is known to have met Emma Hamilton here, whilst his ship was anchored off Teignmouth. We know this because there are letters on display in Torquay museum which bear it out.

One reason for its local fame is that in the eighteenth century a woman resident was murdered in a bedroom, the occasion being recorded for posterity in a drawing made on the spot shortly afterwards. In the 1960s the drawing was bought by the landlord, following complaints by a resident barmaid that she was terrified by an unseen presence in her bedroom. At that time, the licensee was not aware that the bedroom concerned was the room in which the murder took place.

However, round about 1970/71, two television-aerial riggers went into the loft to fit a new aerial. One returned to the landing to act as adviser to his mate, shouting instructions as to the best direction to turn the aerial to obtain a good signal. After some minutes the man in the loft tumbled down the step-ladder, 'his face as white as a sheet and obviously terrified'. He refused to go up again and he also refused, point blank, to tell the licensee what he had seen that had terrified him. The only clue is that the site of his work was directly over the bed in the haunted room below.

I know that today the haunted room is let out as normal accommodation to tourists and holidaymakers, but, so far as I am aware, none has complained or commented on there being any sort of atmosphere in it.

In 1970 the Cambridge University Society for Psychical Research were invited by the licensee of the Golden Lion Hotel, an historic pub on the A1123, about six miles from Huntingdon, to investigate several paranormal events that had taken place there for some length of time. The events that brought things to a head were reported by a man who, whilst staying at the pub, was wakened at two in the morning to find the door, normally fixed with a heavy bolt, swinging wide open and the blankets on his bed pulled off.

Apparently this was no isolated incident, for during his

stay it had occurred three times, and on one occasion, when he was out for the day, a member of the staff saw the ghostly figure of a woman standing inside the bedroom. The door, although previously locked, was found open and the bed disturbed.

These events took place in Room 12, one of the three that have been affected for some time. Room 15, adjoining, is known as 'Cromwell's Room', because it is believed that 'Old Nol' and his officers used it as headquarters during the Civil War. This room houses the ghost of a Cavalier. In 1970 a chambermaid saw the spectral Cavalier outside the room, and a week or so later a guest reported seeing a Cavalier 'which just glided into Room 15'. Blankets are affected in the same way as in Room 12, and two glazed portraits continually fall to the floor – diagonally.

What did the researchers make of it? As is often the case, nothing untoward happened during their stay – but immediately after they had left, bells began ringing, doors opened by themselves and bedclothes were again removed from sleeping guests.

Still in Huntingdonshire, records of the fourteenth-century Bell Inn, which stands just off the A1 – the Great North Road – in the village of Stilton, show that the highwayman Dick Turpin stayed there shortly before his capture. Many and varied are the stories told about this old inn, where strange happenings are still reported today.

A new landlord moved in sometime in 1962. He had not been in long before he decided to leave one of the rooms, in which Dick Turpin is reputed to have slept, empty. It had a strange atmosphere about it, so strange, in fact, that one evening a fire which had been laid in the grate suddenly and for no apparent reason burst into flames!

Early in 1963 the landlord acquired a large dog which began howling soon after midnight and always on a Wednesday – the time when Turpin's ghost is said to walk the old winding passages of the inn. The dog became so distressed that the only solution was to give it tranquillizers to calm it down.

Perhaps the licensee was partly to blame because, for a joke, he had named his dog 'Dick Turpin'.

The Langstone Arms at Chipping Norton made local headlines in the mid-1960s, when noises and an indefinable shape made a bit of a nuisance of itself for several months. The vague form would regularly appear about once every two weeks, heralded by the sound of someone coughing and accompanied by shuffling footsteps. The vague figure resembled that of an elderly woman wearing a veil, which gave rise to the impression that this was the ghost of a nun. She glided along certain corridors of the hotel but was never seen anywhere else. Once she was seen to pass along a corridor and straight through a glass partition. Even sceptics, after hearing first-hand evidence from witnesses, have been known to change their attitude, but although the local historical society investigated the pub's 130-year background, they were unable to trace any record of a murder or suicide which might account for the ghost.

A former chef recalled three encounters with the pub ghost in the 1950s. He said that his first brush with it came when he was in the cellar and he heard a female voice say, 'Fred would not do it like that!' The second meeting came when he returned to the hotel late one night and on entering the kitchen heard a voice say, 'Your supper is on the table!' He went up to his room and found that a meal had been left for him on his bedside table! But the last straw came when, on New Year's Day 1954, he returned from a party and saw the kitchen door open and the figure of a good-looking woman standing there. When he asked her what she wanted, he heard her reply, 'A good night's rest like you are going to have!'

Needless to say, he left the hotel soon after that experience.

Still in Oxfordshire, the Bull Inn at Henley-on-Thames has been the scene of some peculiar incidents over the years. There has been, from time to time, the inexplicable smell of burnt candles in one area of the bar. It is thought there may have been a separate room or passageway through there, prior to alterations many years ago. One occupant reported seeing a cowled figure bending over him while he was in bed, although it has to be said that others who have slept in the room since have never been disturbed.

When, during the Civil War, Chichester fell after a short siege, there was a flood of activity in Siddlesham, a busy little Sussex port some five miles away. It became an important staging-post for Royalists escaping to the Netherlands, and an old inn which stood on the site of the present Crab and Lobster became a centre of undercover operations.

Five Cavaliers, waiting at the tavern for a boat, were surprised one day by a Roundhead patrol, and in a running fight with the troopers, all five were shot down in the roadway outside. They were carried into the inn but died for want of attention to their wounds. For many years there were reports of a tall figure in a dark cloak and tight-fitting clothes, often seen drifting around inside and outside the inn. But in 1965 the haunting became much more credible.

A new landlord had taken over, and from day one his cat began to behave oddly, particularly in the saloon, where it always appeared to avoid certain parts of the floor, often leaping onto a chair in terror, as if trying to avoid something invisible to the people present. Heavy footsteps prowled around the ground-floor rooms at night, despite the place being securely locked up, but whenever the landlord went to investigate, everything was quiet and as it should be. An upstairs room had to be abandoned because of an unpleasant atmosphere.

One summer day in 1969, a man and his wife called at the Crab and Lobster for lunch. As they went through to the dining-room, the lady gasped loudly and stood frozen, gazing into the saloon bar. Later she enquired whether the place was haunted and, when asked why, replied that she had looked into the saloon and seen a man in Cavalier costume lying on the floor, obviously bleeding to death.

He was struggling feebly to staunch the flow of blood from a wound to his chest with a small lace handkerchief. Around him, holidaymakers sat drinking quite oblivious.

Let us now move to the other end of the country and the Maryport Working Men's Club, at Maryport in Cumbria. A few years ago a ghostly girl was seen in the cellars by a barman as he was connecting up a barrel of beer. He returned to the bar with his hair literally standing on end, and after he had recovered from the shock, he told his colleagues that, as he was fixing the beer tap to the barrel, he felt compelled to look up and saw, to his horror, the figure of a girl walk through the wall and into the cellar. He said she paused for a few seconds and then turned and walked back through the wall.

Some nights later she was sighted again by a different member of the staff – the same ghostly woman walked through the wall and repeated the routine of pausing for a second or two, before walking back again through the same wall.

Two young friends, Lisa Donachy and Clare Calhoun of Maryport, came up with a possible explanation as to the identity of the young woman. Many years ago, there stood on the site of the working men's club a boxing parlour owned by a family called Fulton. Their young daughter appears to have suffered from consumption and depression. One day she went out for a walk and was never seen again. It is thought that, in one of her depressive moods, while walking along the promenade at Maryport she decided to end her life and walked fully clothed into the sea and drowned, her body being carried out to sea by the tide.

Whether or not this is what happened is pure conjecture, but the ghostly woman seen in the cellar of the club is described as wearing clothes said to be similar to those worn by the Fulton girl on the day she disappeared.

The Lord Crewe Arms at Blanchland, about twenty-five miles from Newcastle-on-Tyne, is haunted by the ghost of Dorothy Forster. There were two Dorothy Forsters: one was the sister of Tom Forster who plotted the Rebellion in 1715, and the other was her aunt who, at the age of twenty-one, married the seventy-nine-year-old Lord Crewe, Bishop of Durham. Which one haunts the inn is anybody's guess.

Visitors wishing to see the haunted area pass through a massive doorway at the top of a flight of stone steps. The huge door was recently discovered to have been the original inn sign, and it was only after careful cleaning that Lord Crewe's coat-of-arms was revealed.

In December 1968 a woman visitor from Canada staying at the hotel said she not only was conscious of a presence in her bedroom but had felt a thump at the bottom of the bed which she described as 'as though a heavy cat had silently leapt up and tramped across my feet a few times, looking for a place to settle, then decided to jump off'.

One morning shortly afterwards, a chambermaid, having just completed the tidying-up of the affected room, turned round to check she had dealt with everything and was astonished to see that the neat, fresh linen on the bed had been pulled apart and was now heaped in disarray, despite the fact that she had been alone in the room.

When Tom Busby married the daughter of Daniel Auty, a well-known eighteenth-century counterfeiter, he became Auty's partner-in-crime. One day, during an argument over how the money should be shared, Busby lost his temper and beat his father-in-law to death with a hammer. For this, in 1702 he was hanged and gibbeted across from what is today the Busby Stoop Inn, about eight miles from Northallerton in North Yorkshire.

Inside the inn is a chair which, until recent years, stood next to the piano. It was a brave or foolish man who would dare to sit on it − for it was reserved for Tom Busby's ghost! Whoever sat in the chair would be cursed by the ghost and die within a few weeks.

Not convinced? The legend may be odd and a little vague, but it is on record that in the last 200 years death has struck anyone who dared to sit in the chair within a very short time. Many people were dead within days, even hours, and so concerned were the brewery that they eventually had the chair removed out of harm's way. Some of the victims over the past couple of decades have included a fighter pilot from RAF Leeming, killed the day after sitting in the chair; a motorist who crashed the next day and died of his injuries; a motor-cyclist, killed within minutes of leaving the pub; a hitch-hiker, knocked down and killed two days later, and a local man in his late thirties, who died of a massive heart attack the following night.

I will admit that these may all have fallen into the 'high risk' category anyway, but the odds against all of them dying so soon after sitting in Tom Busby's chair – or 'stoop' – must be high enough to suggest that this was no eerie coincidence.

The Crown Hotel at Askern, near Doncaster in South Yorkshire, has a room which is haunted and which frightened the life out of Mrs Banks of Barnsley some years ago.

She told me that, when she was in her teens, her parents were the licensees of the Crown and she had a bedroom on the first floor, directly at the foot of the stairs leading to the second-floor landing. The second floor consisted of bedrooms and a bathroom, and at the end of the corridor was what she describes as 'the room'.

She said: 'Although the other rooms on the second floor were in constant use with bed and breakfast clientele and had been in use for many years before we moved in, the room in question had not been used and, by the look of it, had never been opened in years.' It was full of junk and covered with dust. As she had such a small room on the first floor, Mrs Banks asked her mother if this room could be cleared out for her. She continued: 'My mother agreed and we set to work clearing it out and decorating. Pleased with the finished result, I moved my belongings into my new room – a room, I might add, in which I was to spend only one night.'

That night, eagerly contemplating the delights of a larger, newly decorated bedroom, she went to bed happily and was soon asleep. Normally, once asleep, she never woke until she was called the next morning, but on that night she was awakened by the most strange feeling. Mrs Banks said: 'It may sound odd to say I was wakened by a feeling, as one is normally wakened by a sound, but there was no sound, only the strangest feeling of not being alone, of being watched. It was a most uneasy atmosphere.

For some unknown reason she looked over towards the windows and the heavy curtains blocking out the light, when suddenly and without warning the curtains began to open. 'I can see them now,' she said, 'slowly drawing across the window and flooding the room with moonlight. I can still hear them, the only sound in that strange atmosphere, the sound of curtain runners on the rail, as they worked together to open the curtains.'

Who or what opened the curtains Mrs Banks did not wait to find out. She fled in panic, for as the room filled with moonlight she could see she was still alone. She spent the remainder of the night sitting on the bed in her old room, with the light on. Her brother found her the following morning, still sitting there. After she had told him of her terrifying experience, he pointed out to her that he thought it was strange that the windows to the room were barred and that there was a large lock and two big bolts on the *outside* of the bedroom door.

The pub is over 200 years old and, although it has not been possible to discover who haunts it, or why, one thing is certain: whoever or whatever was locked in that room, someone had tried to make sure it never got out!

York must be the most haunted city in Britain, and there are certainly enough haunted inns and pubs there to satisfy even the most alcoholic ghost-hunter.

The Anglers Arms is a small, cosy old pub in Goodramgate, and it has its fair share of the city's ghosts. On the top floor is a most elusive spectre which never betrays its presence by even the slightest sound or movement, nor has it ever been seen. Yet its presence is very easy to detect, since the strong, distinctive smell of lavender will waft through the rooms, disappearing as quickly and as mysteriously as it came.

On the first floor, and more particularly on the stairs, is the ghost of a friendly Victorian child. The pub cat often seems to be enjoying itself, playing with an invisible partner and purring round the legs of an unseen figure. A regular customer told me that several years ago there were a number of people who claimed to have seen the ghost of a late-Victorian child, sitting on the stairs and looking down on the more solid drinkers in the bar below.

Yet another ghost lurks in the cellars, a ghost that is neither friendly nor playful. The only entrance to the cellar is through a trap-door behind the bar, yet, suddenly and without any reason whatever, the gas taps which pump beer from cellar to bar are frequently turned off. I'm told that the taps, which are in an area of the cellar which is always 'freezing cold', are turned off with such force by the invisible spirit that it requires some considerable strength to turn them back on again. Obviously the ghost of a teetotaller!

The presence in the cellar is the one which is the most tangible. I'm told that it seems to be a 'creature of great age and intelligence and surrounded by utter evil'. Neither the cat nor the pub dog would ever venture down the cellar, and when the pub is dark and empty, the landlady says she would not go down there 'for all the tea in China'.

The York Arms in High Petergate close to York Minster has an industrious but rather timid spirit who has made herself visible once or twice over the years but who seems happiest when she is invisible. When the figure does show herself, she appears as a grey blur which some people say resembles an old or veiled lady. This gives rise to the belief that the mysterious figure is the famous 'Grey Lady' who inhabits the Theatre Royal and that the ghostly meanderings of the long-dead nun take her from the theatre and along Petergate to the Minster. Whoever she is, she is a stickler for tidiness and has an annoying habit of moving objects around.

On one memorable occasion, an old pair of bellows unhooked themselves from the wall, rose upwards to avoid an ornamental plate and glided lazily to the ground, several yards away. I'm told that this caused a sudden rush to the bar and several demands for stiff whiskeys. Numerous small objects, such as cutlery and cassettes, have been thrown about the place, while doors open and close of their own accord. Once the phantom opened the door to the bathroom when the licensee was taking a bath – and she was polite enough hastily to close it again.

In recent years, a small ornament on an upstairs window ledge seemed to interest the ghost. The ornament slid up and down the length of the ledge again and again. The window itself slammed shut, and at the same time a family portrait crashed to the floor. However, the old pub continues to thrive, and the ghost has never been known to harm either occupants or customers.

At Edgeworth in Greater Manchester, the Toby Inn is now thought to be haunted, following curious bumps and other night-time noises which came to a head in the mid-1970s, when the licensee revealed that he had a photograph which clearly shows a ghostly presence. When he first saw the photograph, taken by a customer, he noticed nothing at all unusual, but since then the bar has been altered and when he and his wife were comparing how things were and how they had been, she pointed out on the photograph the figure of a leering man standing at the back of the bar.

But even before the strange affair of the photograph, the landlord had noticed odd noises in the old inn after it had closed, and a number of customers claimed they had seen inexplicable figures in and around the place during opening hours. Although the photograph in itself proves nothing, it is more than a little interesting when one learns that a previous landlord strangled himself after falling out of bed one night, and another licensee collapsed and died of a heart attack, just a foot or so away from where the leering figure is seen on the unusual and puzzling photograph.

The Railway Hotel at Waterfoot in Lancashire's Rossendale Valley stands on the A6066 Rawtenstall to Bacup road, some ten miles from Rochdale. There is no railway here any more, but the pub serves as a reminder of the days of Edwardian steam-trains when they did have a station in the area.

For a number of years the pub has been haunted by the ghost of a woman, known to all as 'Jane', who walks through walls, drifts across bedroom floors and acts in a rather bizarre fashion by removing bedclothes. (Isn't it amazing how many pub spectres seem to show an unhealthy interest in bedclothes?) Quite a number of people who stayed at the pub in the 1960s complained of having their bedclothes removed during the night, and one guest not only suffered the indignity of having his bedding removed by the ghost but actually saw her walk across his bedroom floor and straight through a partitioning wall.

Licensees and their wives have often heard their names being called by a woman, usually when they have been in the tap-room. No one knows who 'Jane' was, but there may be a clue in a bricked-up room at the top of the building. The present landlord refused to discuss it with me.

The White Hart Inn at Caldmore Green in Walsall, Staffordshire, has a haunted attic where a mummified baby's arm was once found. Today this grisly relic is in the safe-keeping of the Walsall Central Library and used to be shown on request. It was found in 1870, alongside a seventeenth-century sword, and is associated with a young woman who is known to have committed suicide at the White Hart some 150 years ago and whose ghost now haunts the old place.

In 1955 the landlord heard curious noises and cries which appeared to come from the attic, and when he investigated he discovered the imprint of a tiny hand on a dust-covered table in one of the attic rooms. He had heard the noises before and thought there would be a logical explanation, but after his visit to the attic and having heard the evidence of a former licensee's wife, who woke up one night to find a white form standing by her bed, his logic began to waver.

A few years later, a relief manager told the local newspaper that on one occasion, while sitting in the living-room immediately below the haunted room, he had heard someone slowly pacing the floor of the empty room above him. He said that the pub dog was looking up the stairs, bristling and growling. Members of a psychical research society once spent a night in the haunted attic, and although nothing was seen, the atmosphere indicated the existence of something paranormal and the temperature was much colder than it should have been.

The mummified arm, though, is something of a mystery, because it has now been established that it is a hospital specimen which has been injected with a preservative. This leaves one to suggest that both the arm and the sword were in some way connected with witchcraft, rather than with the ghost of the young woman.

One often hears cases of people encountering a ghost almost immediately on moving into premises, and such a case occurred in Kidderminster in 1963, which was unusual in that before that date there was no traditional story to explain the sudden haunting.

Within weeks of taking over Harvey's Wine Bar in Swan Street, Kidderminster, the licensee began to hear footsteps when there was no one in the building other than himself. Then a series of uncanny events occurred: mysterious bangings, doors opening and closing of their own accord and other little incidents which prompted the licensee to stay no longer than was absolutely necessary once the bar had closed each night.

One evening a customer was sitting alone in a room at the back of the wine bar when one of the doors suddenly opened and closed, then the latch of another door which led out into the street was raised, the door opened by itself – against the spring – and quietly closed. It was as if someone had entered the room, walked casually across to the other side and then left by the other door. No doubt the customer went on the waggon after that!

A short time afterwards, a barmaid actually saw the

ghost one afternoon as she cleared up after closing-time. She suddenly heard footsteps and, thinking someone had been locked in by accident, went to check. There was no one there, but as she turned to go back to the bar, she was surprised to see the figure of a woman suddenly coming round the bar towards her. She later described the figure as young and tall and dressed very smartly. She was wearing a long brown dress which was pulled in tightly at the waist, and with a ruffled collar. On her head she wore a straw bonnet. The barmaid still thought she was a customer, until she realized that the clothes were several centuries out of date. She said she was not in the least afraid, as the figure smiled in a friendly way before drifting past and disappearing through a side door.

After a second barmaid was terrified on encountering the lady in the brown dress some weeks later, it was decided that they really ought to try to discover something about her which might give a clue as to why she haunted the building. The clue seemed to lie in the wine cellar, something which was uncovered by the *Kidderminster Times*, which took up the story.

It appears that Harvey's Wine Bar is built on the site of the former Clarence Inn. In 1851, when the inn's stable flooring was being repaired, it gave way, disclosing a great vault below which contained a two-foot-deep layer of decayed animal matter and human bones. On-the-spot investigations revealed that the vault had probably been filled with human remains and then covered over, for the bricks of the arch were of a much later date. Sifting through the grim find, the investigators discovered a small black bottle, an old drinking-glass, a clumsy pick-axe and some unusually shaped and rather heavy tobacco pipes.

Historians believe that the vault, which had a pointed roof and sixteenth-century mullioned windows, could have been a chapel which had belonged to a private manor house nearby. Whether there was any connection between the human remains and the brown-clad lady or the chapel, no one really knows. It was another mystery which only adds to the fascination of these old inns and pubs.

*

For our final ghost in this chapter, let us return to London and one of its most famous haunted pubs, the Grenadier, which stands in the Old Barracks Yard, off Wilton Row near Marble Arch. This pub began life in the eighteenth century as an officers' mess for the Coldstream Guards and the Grenadier Guards. In those days, one of the bars was situated in what are today the cellars, and the present bar was, in fact, the officers' dining-room.

In the early nineteenth century, a young officer was allegedly caught cheating at cards and was horse-whipped so badly by his fellow officers that he died after staggering down the steps into the cellar. Although documentary evidence regarding this incident is fragmentary, there is good reason to believe that the incident did take place around 1820 and that none other than the Duke of Wellington was involved in the subsequent cover-up.

There is no record of the month in which the incident took place but, according to reports which go back well into the last century, it is always in September when most of the incidents occur – incidents which include an icy coldness in the cellar, the sensation of an invisible body bumping violently into bystanders, and a variety of unusual noises. On one occasion in the 1970s, a barman was struck by an antique military helmet that hurtled from its place on the wall; a cellarman was grabbed by a powerful and unseen hand and pulled backwards down the cellar steps.

One September a young boy lying in bed with the door open saw what he later described as a shadow of someone on the landing. As he watched, it grew larger and larger before becoming smaller again, as though someone was approaching the bedroom and then retreating. One licensee's wife, changing in her bedroom just before opening at lunchtime and believing herself alone in that part of the pub, didn't bother to close the door. Suddenly, when she was still half-naked, she became aware of a man climbing the stairs towards her bedroom. Quickly grabbing something to cover herself, she turned to confront the intruder, only to find there was no one there at all. She did not recognize the figure she had caught a quick glimpse of, but she was later assured that no one had been in that area of the pub at the time.

Another time, a woman having a drink at the bar distinctly saw a man going up the same stairway, who disappeared as if into thin air before reaching the top.

10. Spectral Workmates

It was just after one o'clock in the morning. Twenty-three-year-old coal-miner Stephen Dimbleby was beginning a shift, due to end at dawn. Some 3,000 feet below ground, he trudged towards a man-made tunnel about fourteen or fifteen feet wide, carrying his duffel-bag containing his sandwiches and water bottle. All was silent as he approached the tunnel; the only sound was the crunch of his heavy boots on the rocky floor. The only light came from his lamp fastened to the front of his miner's helmet. Ahead of him, he could see the faint glow of lights as two of his colleagues vanished into the tunnel several yards in front.

Stephen is a pleasant, likeable young man who has worked down Rotherham's Silverwood Colliery since leaving school. Even though it can be tiring, back-breaking work, the rewards are good, and he considered it a challenge. Until that night in March 1982, he had always been something of a happy-go-lucky person.

In the past his mates had tried to frighten him with tales that the pit was haunted. It is on record that in the late 1960s a miner had died, horribly mutilated, when he was caught up and dragged into a digging-machine. Now, they said, the victim's restless spirit still lurked in the pit, and strange, inexplicable lights could sometimes be seen. Stephen just laughed at the stories, and they were far from his mind when he entered the tunnel. His only thoughts were of his work.

Suddenly, beneath the centre of the arch, the figure of another coal-miner appeared. He didn't seem to have stepped out of the shadows at the side of the tunnel – he

simply materialized. In the underground gloom, Stephen
thought he had been mistaken: no one could suddenly
materialize from nowhere, 3,000 feet below ground. Or
could they? He noticed something rather strange about
the man. He was about Stephen's height and carried the
kind of lamp miners had not used for a number of years.
On his head he wore an old leather-covered safety helmet,
long since replaced by more up-to-date ones. Instead of
the orange overalls pitmen wear today, this man was
dressed in a coal-covered waistcoat, collarless shirt and
baggy trousers.

The stranger raised his lamp and nodded, as if
acknowledging Stephen's presence. But the young miner
saw something else in the glow of his own lamp, which
made him cry out in horror. The face of the man had no
features – no eyes, no nose, no mouth. It was black, but not
with the usual blackness of a collier's face, streaked with
coal dust. This was the blackness of empty space! The
figure itself seemed human enough, and Stephen felt that,
if he touched it, he would feel real flesh and bone. But he
was not prepared to do so. Instead he dropped his bag,
turned and ran to where he knew he would find his mates.

Terrified, he raced screaming across the rocky and
bumpy surface, scrambling and stumbling for much of the
way. Then he saw a pit deputy staring at him in
amazement, and Stephen flung himself at him, crying, 'My
God! I've seen him!' So shocked was Stephen that he had
to be admitted to hospital.

As recently as November 1984, two colliery deputies
reported seeing lights which they found hard to explain.
One said that at about 8.30 p.m. he saw a glow like that
from a miner's helmet-lamp appear on the coal face. It
shone for about ten minutes, but when the deputy went to
investigate, the light disappeared. Some minutes later, the
light re-appeared and glowed for a further ten minutes.

If this is the ghost of a dead coal-miner, it would
certainly not be alien to the well-being of miners working
at Silverwood Colliery today. Perhaps he is there to warn
them of imminent danger. Mining is a tough industry, and
miners are not going to let a mere ghost scare them. Most

just take that sort of thing for granted.

A rather confusing ghost is known to haunt the Birmingham Repertory Theatre's Hire Department in Oozle Street, which a number of people say is that of a woman in medieval costume. But a member of the staff who has had experience of the ghost told me this is not so. The ghost, she claims, is of a woman in modern clothing.

Very often there are a number of funny smells drifting about the building, particularly the dressing-rooms, which, Mrs Lynn Simpson tells me, smell on occasion 'like a gents' lavatory', whilst on several other occasions it smells as though something is on fire. These smells continue off and on for several weeks, and the burning smell in particular causes considerable worry, as can well be imagined in a place which contains several thousand costumes. But although extensive enquiries and searches are made, nothing is ever discovered which could account for it.

Noises are heard in the old building, which dates from the nineteenth century, probably originally a brass foundry. This is more or less confirmed by the presence of Brasshouse Passage, which runs behind the building. When taken over by the Birmingham Repertory Theatre as their costume and hire department, the place had a reputation for being haunted, but no one took it seriously, least of all Mrs Simpson. Then, one busy day, she was standing at the reception desk writing out a hire agreement form when suddenly a young woman passed across reception and appeared to walk into the waiting-room, which at the time was occupied by a gentleman.

Mrs Simpson said: 'As I was writing, I only caught her out of the corner of my eye. She seemed a normal enough person to me. She was dressed in either a dark green or black coat, which at a glance seemed reasonably up-to-date.'

Having finished dealing with her customer, Mrs Simpson went into the waiting-room to see whether the lady had come to meet the gentleman already waiting there. She said: 'Often one person will come in, whilst the other parks the car or something, and then come back to join them. I thought this was the case, but when I went into the waiting-room, there was just the gentleman sitting by himself.' She asked the man where the woman had gone to, and to her surprise he replied, 'What woman? No one has been in here while I have been waiting!' Mrs Simpson thought that perhaps the woman had gone straight through to the changing-rooms or the workshop, but a thorough search of the entire building again revealed nothing.

Since then, nothing else has been seen, although the smells and noises have persisted. It used to be assumed that, if the place was haunted, it would be by someone who had been killed on the premises during its days as a foundry. But the appearance of a strange woman in modern clothing has quashed this theory, and who she is or why she came back to haunt the place is a complete mystery.

Does the reader, like me, work from home? Or perhaps you sometimes have occasion to take some of your work home with you? If so, the experience of Dr Ross may give you food for thought.

Dr Anne Ross is an eminent Celtic scholar and archaeologist who does research work for a number of museums. Late in 1971 she was asked to examine two carved stone heads which had been discovered near Hadrian's Wall, in Northumberland. Although there was nothing at all unpleasant about the appearance of the heads, she took an immediate and instinctive dislike to them. Leaving them in the box they had been sent in, she put them in her study at home for safe-keeping, planning to have them geologically examined and then return them as soon as possible.

A night or two after they had arrived, Dr Ross woke up suddenly at about 2 a.m., deeply frightened and very cold. She glanced towards the bedroom door and, by the corridor light, glimpsed a tall figure slipping out of the room. Her first impression was that the figure was dark, like a shadow, and that it was part animal and part man. Some strange, irresistible force compelled her to get out of bed and follow it.

She heard whatever-it-was going downstairs and then saw it moving along the passage which led to the kitchen; but now she was too terrified to go any further, returning to the bedroom to waken her husband. He searched the house and was unable to find any sign of a disturbance; everything was as it should be, and so Dr Ross agreed she must have had a nightmare and decided to say no more about it.

A few days later, when the house was empty, her teenaged daughter returned from school at a little after 4 p.m., two hours before her mother and father were due to return from London. When they arrived home, they discovered their daughter in a state of shock, and she blurted out to them that something rather terrible had happened, although at first she would not tell them what.

Eventually the whole story came out. When she had first got in from school, she had seen something huge, dark and inhuman on the stairs. It had rushed down towards her, vaulted over the bannister and landed in the corridor with a soft thud, which made her think its feet were padded like those of an animal. The figure had run towards her room and, though she was absolutely terrified, she felt compelled to follow it. At the door it had vanished, leaving the girl in the state in which her parents found her. They calmed her down as best they could and, feeling puzzled and disturbed themselves, searched the house. Again there was no sign of any intruder, nor did they expect to find any.

After that they often felt a cold presence in the house, and more than once heard the soft 'thud' of an animal's pads near the staircase. Several times the door to Dr Ross's study has burst open when there has been no draught or anything else to account for it. On one other occasion, when she and her daughter were going down the stairs together, they both thought they saw a dark figure ahead of them, hearing it land in the corridor after vaulting the bannister.

Had the hauntings anything to do with the stone heads? Dr Ross thinks so. Later she learned that, on the night they had first been discovered, the woman who lived next-door to the garden where they had been unearthed was putting her child to bed when a horrifying creature, which she later described as 'half animal, half man', came into the room. She began to scream and only stopped when the neighbours came running. She was convinced the creature had touched her, but what had happened to it after that, or where it had gone, she had no idea. Again, there was no sign that anyone had broken into the house, and the incident, like the incidents which had taken place in the Ross household, was without any rational explanation. It is strange that, although the heads were later returned to the museum, the 'thing' – or whatever it is – does not appear to have gone with them.

Later examination of the heads showed that they were carved from local Northumbrian stone, probably during the Romano-British period, about 1,800 years ago. They might have come from a military shrine or temple of the Celtic legionaries who made up a large part of the garrison on Hadrian's Wall. If this was the case, they would have been placed as guardian stones outside the shrine of a local god, such as Maponus, 'the Divine Son', a hunting god who is known to have been worshipped in the northern counties of Britain.

Similar carvings have been found all over Europe; the Celts were head-hunters, who believed that the severed human head had magical and divine powers. The heads of enemies were buried beneath altar stones, nailed to the gateposts of their forts or thrown into wells, where they were thought to convey fertility and ward off evil powers.

Powers such as these would have been vested in the stylized stone heads and, once, those which had been sent to Dr Ross for examination may have stood guard over a god who has long since departed. Or has he?

There used to stand, in London's Euston Road, a funeral director's parlour and mortuary, which today has been replaced by the premises of the independent radio station

Capital Radio, which beams out music and information throughout the night, to cater mainly for night workers and insomniacs.

During these all-night programmes, the presenter is usually alone in the small studio, which has a glass port into the master control room, where the engineers work to keep the programmes on the air. Normally, apart from the presenter and engineers, the only other persons in the building are the security men at the main door and a young woman who mans the switchboard for Capital Radio's 'Helpline'.

Just before Christmas 1977, a presenter on the all-night spot was actually on the air, talking between records, when suddenly he heard what he later described as a dull 'clunk', as if someone was at the door of the studio and knocking to get in. The engineers also heard it. The presenter hesitated (a hesitation which didn't go unnoticed by the listeners), thinking to himself that no one in their right mind would walk into the studio whilst the red light was on and he was on the air.

Through the glass port, he could see the engineers, and he thought it a bit unusual that they had not at least attempted to stop whoever was now trying the door. The presenter heard the large door, which had its own distinctive sound, open. But no one came into the studio. Then he heard footsteps seemingly move away again. It was unusual, to say the least. The security men were still downstairs, and the engineers were sitting, as before, in the control room, yet there was a definite sound of someone trying to get into the studio. He was sure it was a real person, and it was only afterwards that he realized there was something very odd about the whole incident.

So far as I have been able to discover, as few people at Capital Radio seem inclined to want to discuss it, the noises and footsteps have not been heard for about six or seven years. Perhaps it was a 'one-off' type of experience which happens from time to time, or perhaps it had something to do with the undertaker's parlour. I don't know. I suppose it is only natural that many radio and television stations are reluctant to discuss, or even admit to, the presence of a ghost on their premises. But from time to time odd stories do get out, although unfortunately the attitude of the authorities often precludes one's following them up.

Typical are the studios of Granada Television at Manchester, where they are said to have a haunted dressing-room, and the one-time theatre at Chatham, now used as a studio by Television South, which is said to be haunted by a woman who was once seen walking up a wide stairway and who is probably connected with the old theatre. The Southcote Road studios of the independent local radio station Two Counties Radio, at Bournemouth, is another site which has been the scene of ghostly episodes, and a ghost at the Plymouth studios of Television South West actually drove at least one employee into resigning on the spot.

In Eastgate Street in the centre of Chester there stands an old shop, a branch of Finlay's tobacconists. No one knows exactly why it is haunted, but the theory is that the ghostly goings-on are associated with a suicide which took place on the premises some hundred years ago.

On several occasions over the years, staff have heard someone enter the shop, yet no one is seen, not even when an assistant is behind the counter. One disturbing aspect of this haunting is an unusual wailing which seems to originate in the centre of the shop floor and which has been heard by staff and customers alike. 'It sounds,' I was told, 'like a woman moaning.' Heavy thumps and stamping sounds have also been heard several times, which appear to come from a room above the sales area, and often, when staff have gone to this room, they have heard footsteps following them.

Things became so bad that in the 1970s an exorcism had to be performed, and the pitiful cries, although still heard on occasion, are not as frequent today. I understand that many years ago this used to be a glassware shop, and during that time the shopkeeper's wife hanged herself after her husband deserted her. Before that, there was an old burial ground on the site.

Even today, doors still open by themselves and lights go

off and on for no apparent reason, but the ghost has been accepted as a fact of life by the staff. There is a feeling of peace and friendliness about the place today, and the staff are confident that the ghost means them no harm.

Alongside Marks & Spencer in Burnley is Bethesda Street where for over 150 years there has stood a chapel. Beside the chapel there used to be a Sunday School and a small graveyard. Sometime during the 1950s the Sunday School was demolished and the graveyard was built over, so that today the chapel stands sandwiched between a modern office block and a fairly large shop.

The fact that the shop is said to be haunted leads many people to believe that, unknown to the developers, some remains had been buried in the old Sunday School building and may have been left under the site. Whatever the reason, prior to the opening of the shop in July 1978, rumour began to circulate that things were not quite what they should be. A fitter was repairing a window at the front of the building, alone in the shop, when he suddenly heard voices coming from a store-room. The voices were muffled and he was unable to discern what was being said, but on investigation he was startled to discover that there was no one else there. Returning to the front of the shop, he was even more amazed to find that all the doors had been mysteriously locked behind him. Gas and Electricity Board workers also complained of inexplicable happenings, and people soon began to think that there was indeed something odd about the place.

It was enough to disturb anyone who went into the building, least of all the staff. Alarm bells ring after they have been turned off; light bulbs appear from nowhere and smash on the floor; the lift stops quite suddenly and for no apparent reason, and no electrical fault can be discovered which might cause it to happen.

One of the biggest scares came in July 1978, when three receptionists of Trident Discount, who were then the occupiers, were in the front shop when they heard a terrific crash coming from a small store-room. The door was locked, so it was not possible for there to have been anyone in there. Investigation revealed two shattered lights bulbs on the floor – nothing at all unusual in that, you might think, especially as this was an electrical store, yet one thing puzzled the investigators: the type of bulbs that were smashed were of a pre-war manufacture, unlike any that are sold today. To this day no one knows where the bulbs came from. The manager, checking the boiler room, which leads off from the store-room, was surprised when another of these pre-war bulbs appeared to roll, as if from nowhere, into the middle of the floor.

Another noticeable fact was that the temperature was always markedly lower in this small store-room than in any other part of the building, when everywhere should be of a constant temperature. On another occasion, when the store-room door was opened, it was discovered that a vacuum hose and a calculator had been moved. It was certain that no member of the staff had been in there – and the most mystifying thing of all was that, when someone went to pick it up, the vacuum hose was red hot!

During the peak Christmas shopping period a few years ago, assistants in a shoe shop in Wisbech High Street in Cambridgeshire constantly claimed to have heard strange sounds – footsteps on the stairs and in the rooms above the shop. Lights were being turned off and on during the night, and when the floor of an unused room was sprinkled with talcum powder to check if it had been walked on, small footprints were discovered when it was opened up the following morning.

Local theory is that this is activity caused by the uneasy ghost of Queen Anne Boleyn, for history shows that, during the time she was courting Henry VIII, she entertained him at Wisbech, as well as at nearby Blickling Hall in Norfolk. Legend says that she haunts both places round about Christmastime.

Similarly, a smart hairdressing salon in Hull was the subject of the attention of an anonymous and noisy ghost which caused quite a stir in the town in 1972. The salon stood in Whitefriargate, not far from Paragon Station in the city centre. At the time the owners were a Mr and Mrs Hardy, who had become so disturbed, late in 1971, by mysterious noises coming from an upstairs room that they called the police. The sounds, which had been heard by both staff and customers, were those of someone slowly pacing the floor of the empty room and dragging something towards the door, followed by further shuffling and scuffling.

The police had to admit that they were baffled by it all, but they locked the door and fitted trip-wires etc. They were even more baffled when the sounds continued and when, on opening up the room, they found it remained undisturbed, although the lights had been mysteriously switched on. Investigations by the police, local press and others have failed to bring to light any reasonable explanation for the unaccountable noises, which, so far as I am aware, continue to this day.

That much-loved and respected character actor Arthur Lucan, was a big draw at theatres and cinemas wherever he appeared, with his wife and partner, Kitty McShane, as 'Old Mother Riley and her daughter, Kitty'. He collapsed and died in his dressing-room at the Tivoli Theatre at Hull on 17 May 1954, just a week before he was due to attend a meeting with local tax inspectors.

The 'Old Mother Riley' character was a great favourite with the kids of my generation, and it is perhaps fitting that Arthur Lucan's grave in the East Cemetery at Hull is nearly always covered with flowers, put there by children who never knew him but have seen his films on television – a touching reminder of the happiness he brought through his famous character, even though he himself had known nothing but unhappiness most of his life.

Alas, like Arthur, the Tivoli has gone too, closing down as a theatre not long after his death. It was finally pulled down in 1959, and ironically an Income Tax office was built on the site. Now it appears that Arthur Lucan is taking his revenge on the people who had hounded him for many years, for I have it on good authority that his ghost, dressed in his 'Old Mother Riley' costume, has been seen on several occasions by Inland Revenue staff. An Inland Revenue official told me: 'We don't like to say too much about what Arthur Lucan is up to, although members of staff do tend to stay away from a certain store-room on the second floor.'

He also agreed that the ghost of 'Old Mother Riley' has been seen in the building and that there is a very strange atmosphere about the place sometimes.

A terrifying and rather grizzly experience befell a well-known Brighton antiquarian bookseller some years ago. He had been told that there was a hoard of old books in the basement of a junk shop in Edward Street, a part of the town that was developed in the early nineteenth century. He found the books in what appeared to have been, at one time, the old kitchen – a murky, desolate place which did not even boast an electric light. His attention was drawn to an alcove in which was a large old stone sink whose shape reminded him of an old-fashioned coffin. Above the alcove was an archway of small blood-red bricks, set in a curious zigzag pattern. The place had a horrible eerie atmosphere about it, and had it not been for the promising collection of saleable old books which were stored there, the man later admitted that he doubted if he would have stayed.

It was getting towards evening and the owner of the junk shop, who knew him, told him that he never remained in the place after dark. He gave him the keys, telling him to look through the books at his leisure and then lock the place up when he was finished. Armed with a paraffin lamp, a flask of coffee and some sandwiches, the antiquarian settled down in the gloomy basement and began to browse through some of the fascinating old books he had found there, oblivious to the deep, oppressive silence.

He said: 'After about an hour, a macabre chill feeling began to creep over me. Not only did it begin to feel cold, but there was also now an atmosphere of evil, which made me feel a little uneasy. The books now seemed to lose all interest to me and I began to feel that I was not alone in that silent kitchen with its coffin-like sink, lit only by the feeble light of my paraffin lamp. Someone, or something, was in there with me, watching!'

Unable to stand the oppressive atmosphere any longer, he suddenly stood up, looking towards the archway as he did so, and to his absolute horror he saw a fat, naked woman standing beside that dreadful sink. He continued: 'She was obese, almost shapeless, with the face of someone long dead. The eyeless sockets and cheeks falling into decay. Her limbs were swollen and blotched in an appalling manner, and she hovered beside the great sink, her eyeless sockets fixed on me.'

He happened to be holding a large volume in his hand and, with sudden panic, threw it at the apparition. The book went straight through her and hit the archway behind. Then, slowly and with a look of malevolence on her face, the woman disappeared. Quickly gathering his belongings, the bookseller left in a hurry, no longer interested in the old books. He had arranged to leave the keys with a woman who lived in a flat above the shop. When he knocked on her door, she exclaimed, 'Goodness me! You look as if you've seen a ghost. Have you been down in the shop basement alone?' She went on to say that the shopkeeper had no right to leave him down there on his own after dark. 'I asked her what was down there that was so frightening,' he said. 'She told me that the basement had been haunted for well over eighty years and that she herself had once met the ghost on the cellar stairs, and it had walked right through her.'

Research has revealed that about ninety years ago a man who lived on the premises had murdered his wife in that kitchen, and he had then begun to dismember her body in that very same old sink, the object being to bury the remains under the stone floor. As it happened, a neighbour had heard the woman's screams and had alerted the police. They were too late to prevent the murder, but they caught the man in the act of cutting up his wife's body. It goes without saying that he was later hanged for the crime.

*

There are probably as many haunted factories and warehouses in England as there are haunted pubs, if we are to believe all the claims which have been made over the years.

In 1923 a tragic accident occurred at Darlington & Simpson's Rolling Mills in Durham, when an overhead cable railway broke, killing six men working under it and injuring several more. Ever since that day, numerous workers claim to have been disturbed by 'vague shapes' in the area where the accident happened. Then, in mid-1970, a group of men saw what they described as 'a transparent shape' gliding swiftly across the huge floor of the finishing-mill. It vanished through a wall leading to an adjoining site.

Quickly following the figure outside, the men ran into the road and saw the apparition perched on top of the wall, where it appeared to lose its balance and then vanished. Several of the men thought the shape might have been smoke from a nearby chimney, but they later realized that it was first seen inside the factory.

Local theory is that this is the ghost of one of the young workers who was killed in the cable railway accident, for during his refreshment breaks he had sometimes scrambled onto the wall to give impromptu gymnastic displays to his amused colleagues. Apparently the showing-off came to an abrupt end one day, when he fell from the wall and broke a leg.

Another factory ghost pops up at Standish, near Wigan. Over a period of about four years, several unexplained happenings at that old Lancashire cotton mill culminated in a rather bizarre incident, one night in 1963, causing a nineteen-year-old cloth-roller at the mill to faint with shock. On his recovery, he said he had looked up from his machine and saw a figure in a long coat floating in the air a couple of feet above the factory floor. The phantom wore old-fashioned knickerbockers and seemed to have a white scarf tied around its neck.

Although he was unaware of the fact, the terrified worker had seen the ghost of the Reverend Charles

Newton Hutton, who had been rector of Standish for fifty years and who had died in 1938. Older residents of the area still remember him: short-necked, bearded and invariably wearing gaiters. Today the old rector's ghost still haunts the village, although he is harmless enough.

Apparently the mill was erected on land which had once belonged to the Hutton family, and Mr Hutton had had a financial interest in it during his lifetime, often visiting the mill.

One odd aspect of this story is that, by a remarkable coincidence, the appearance of the apparition to the mill machinist occurred the day before Mr Hutton's widow died.

The famous old Brooklands racetrack at Weybridge in Surrey is now derelict, but part of the circuit is covered by buildings which belong to British Aerospace. One vast assembly shed, known as 'the Vatican', juts out into the former racetrack at the end of the Railway Straight and is reputed to be haunted by the ghost of Percy Lambert, a renowned and popular motor-racing figure in his day. During a record attempt in his Talbot, a tyre burst, throwing him and his machine towards where the huge assembly works now stand, and today both the sound and spectre of his car, complete with Percy Lambert at the wheel, have been experienced quite frequently on the site at varying times of the day and night.

One evening in the 1970s a mechanic heard the sound of Lambert's car and turned round in time to see what he described as 'a misty shape of the old vehicle pass the doors of the Vatican'. He said he could distinctly make out a figure behind the wheel, wearing a skullcap and goggles. After travelling about fifty yards, the phantom vanished.

In 1963 several workers at the factory stated that they had seen the ghost dressed in a helmet and leather coat of the style worn by a 1920s racing driver.

At the firm of Johnsons, the famous furniture cream manufacturers, near Camberley in Surrey, two factory cleaners reported in 1971 that, while cleaning on the mezzanine floor late at night, they had seen the figure of a man dressed in black standing watching them. They said that his outline had appeared hazy and indistinct, and when one of them had said 'Hello?', the figure simply disappeared. Later other members of staff claimed that they too had seen the ghost and had thought it was a man until it suddenly vanished. This figure has always been seen in the same place, on the mezzanine floor, quite harmlessly watching what is going on.

I understand that the building is of fairly modern construction, but it is thought to have been erected on the site of old farm buildings. It appears that one of the building workers is known to have died during the construction of Johnsons, and it is thought to be his ghost which is seen quite regularly.

The Mobil Oil Refinery at Coryton, a few miles from Southend-on-Sea, was once owned by the fuel-distributing firm of Cory Bros. During that time, one of their workers accidentally fell to his death in the oily sludge of a separator tank during his nightly tour of inspection. Since then the unfortunate man's ghost has been seen on the site by several Mobil workers.

One night early in 1970, a maintenance man was sheltering from the cold wind blowing off the Thames. He was sitting in the cab of a fuel bowser, a small petrol tanker parked near what is known as the 'tank farm' when he heard footsteps echoing along the roadway towards one of the separator units. (This equipment is used to clean the water used in various processes before returning it to the River Thames.) He wondered who could be strolling around at that time of night, and called out, enquiring who was there.

There was no reply, but the footsteps moved nearer and he saw, in the glare of one of the road lamps, the figure of a stout man, wearing a boilersuit and a white steel helmet. The figure continued to walk on beside the gulley which surrounds the site, until he was less than fifteen feet from the fuel bowser. The maintenance man jumped down from the cab, calling out – but as the figure turned to cross the roadway, it simply vanished.

Consett, on the A68, about fifteen miles north-west of Durham, was, at the turn of the century, the centre of a thriving industrial complex. One of the biggest employers in Consett at that time was a paper mill which stood at the end of Spring Lane.

Among the many workers who regularly walked to the mill each day was a young man called Jack Arthur, who would set out from his lodgings in Snows Green each morning to begin work at 7.30. His landlord was the local postman, who found this arrangement ideal, for they left the house at the same time each morning, and on finishing his round he was able to get back home in good time to prepare an evening meal for Jack and himself.

The young mill worker often accompanied the postman part of the way down Spring Lane before they parted, each to his own work, and the arrangement seemed to work quite satisfactorily for both men.

However, after a few months, the difference in their ages began to influence their attitudes. Jack wanted to enjoy himself in his spare time, whilst the postman, a rather staid character, could not understand the frivolous outlook of the lad. So it was not very long before neighbours began to hear rows and arguments between the two. Jack would want to go chasing the girls or lounging in the pub with his mates, while the older man preferred to stay at home with his pigeons.

The atmosphere worsened, and one evening in the winter of 1896 a terrific argument was heard by the neighbours. It appears that the postman was threatening to throw Jack out into the street if he didn't stop his drinking and throwing his money about on the fairer sex. Some locals believe that Jack may have had more money than the postman knew, for it was well known that he was always gambling and could quite easily have afforded to pay more for his keep.

The morning following the heated argument, the

postman was seen on his rounds, but his lodger was never seen again. Numerous enquiries and investigations were made but, despite strong suspicion, no action could be taken. Jack Arthur had simply vanished.

Soon reports began to reach the police of a figure resembling the young mill worker having been seen in Spring Lane, but further searches of the area revealed nothing, and in time the incident was forgotten.

Then the affair was resurrected some seventy years later, when, in December 1970, a local postal worker reported that, while delivering letters at the Snows Green end of Spring Lane at 7.30 in the morning, she had had an overwhelming sensation that she was being watched. The morning was dark and cold and the lonely stretch of road had a terrifying atmosphere about it. The postal worker had been delivering letters on that route for a long time, but she had never experienced that terrifying feeling before. In fact, she was so afraid that she was transferred to a different round.

Four days later the new postman for the area rushed into the sorting office and stammered out that he had seen the ghost of a young man, standing no more than a couple of yards away, silently watching him. The location was exactly where the previous postal worker had been terrified, and the description of the ghost and the clothes he wore matched those of young Jack Arthur when he disappeared in 1896.

A few weeks later a milkman reported a similar incident, claiming he had seen the figure several times, and over the past few years there have been several other well-authenticated sightings by early morning workers, newspaper boys and the police.

Perhaps one of the strangest and most written-about ghostly phenomena was that which frightened the life out of a gang of demolition workers when they arrived in Southport on Merseyside in 1969 to demolish the old Palace Hotel at Birkside. On the face of it, it appeared a straightforward job for the skilled team, but the demolition men were to find this the oddest and most unnerving one they had ever undertaken.

During periods of quiet on the corridors and in upper rooms, strange whispering was heard; in fact, the whole building had a weird atmosphere about it. But perhaps the most extraordinary feature was the inexplicable behaviour of the lift, which the men were not long in noticing, for it appeared to possess a will of its own – despite the fact that it was without power.

Entering the hotel one morning, nine of the workmen saw the lift doors slide together and watched open-mouthed as it ascended to the second floor. At the time the hotel was deserted and the electricity supply had been cut off for weeks. Investigators from the North West Electricity Board were summoned and were soon to report that there was not an amp of electricity in the whole building. The workmen then ran up to the winding-room to investigate, and they discovered that the brake on the lift winding-drum was still in its 'on' position, which, under normal circumstances, should have prevented the lift from moving either up or down.

Dumbfounded at the uncanny performance of the lift, which appeared to have been motivated by some unknown agency, they cut through the one-inch-thick cables which supported it. The lift stayed where it was. They cut through the cables supporting the counter-balance, but still the lift stubbornly refused to move, though there was nothing to hold it. Finally they used heavy hammers and crowbars with all the human energy possible to prise away the lift's guide bars before the four-ton car finally plunged to the pit at the bottom of the shaft, where it buried itself several feet in the ground.

Everyone was mystified. The lift had travelled up and down quite easily of its own accord *and* without power, yet only the greatest human energy could force it into movement, almost smashing the car in the process. The extraordinary affair received a great deal of publicity, the newspapers carrying headlines and interviews with the men concerned. It became a feature on BBC Television, in which those who had witnessed the phenomenon described what they had seen, yet for which they could offer no explanation.

The hotel's 112-year history held no obvious explanation, yet it was quite clear that it was subject to paranormal influences. There were theories, of course (there always are), and one suggested that the original architect of the building had committed suicide by jumping from a top landing, where odd noises and an eerie atmosphere had been reported several times, to fall to his death on the spot where the lift later stood. Also, the hotel had been used as a reception centre for victims of a sea tragedy, some of whom had died there. There were other incidents of a tragic nature connected with the place which had occurred many years before.

Another interesting factor in this story is that it was noticed that no animal could be persuaded to visit the top landing. Time and again one of the demolition men had no difficulty in getting his dog to follow him all over the rest of the building, but whenever he approached the top landing, the dog refused to go further.

The answer to these extraordinary events must lie somewhere in the long train of events buried in the past and almost forgotten. But the demolition team has not forgotten the strange experience, and they were thankful when the job was done and they were well away from the site. As for the ghosts, perhaps they left with the last skip-full of rubbish. Who knows?

And finally. Having read the chapter in which many motorists claim to have seen spectres on the highways of England, it will be of some comfort to the drivers amongst my readers to learn that the Automobile Association boasts its own ghost. They can expect a sympathetic hearing if they meet a spectre on their travels and report it to the AA headquarters in Derby Road, Nottingham.

This ghost affects not only Fanum House but also the store next door, and although during the summer some 3,000 motorists visit the offices each week, to my knowledge the apparition has been seen on only two occasions. Once it was seen by a shift worker at one o'clock in the morning. He thought the figure standing just inside the door was a motorist who had broken down and was seeking some assistance, but as soon as he spoke to the man, asking how he could help, the figure simply vanished. The AA man was so unnerved by the experience that he immediately went to lock the front door – but it was already locked.

Various other incidents have been reported over the past twenty years. Definite footsteps have been heard by all the night staff, walking across the first floor, and in 1971 an ambulance driver was so puzzled at the crashing sounds coming from an upstairs canteen that he dashed into the room, only to discover that it was empty and nothing had been moved.

It appears that Fanum House was built in 1958 on what had once been the local council refuse dump. Just one year after the building was opened, the AA area supervisor collapsed and died at his desk late one afternoon. It is thought to be his hard-working spirit which still haunts his old office – just to make sure that the standards of the Automobile Association are maintained!

11. Black Dogs and Other Animals

Dogs, cats and horses have always been associated with the spirit world. They are said to be able to sense, even see, ghosts which are invisible to the human eye. But some animals exist as four-legged phantoms themselves, and the most terrifying are the black Hounds of Hell. Almost every part of Britain has such animals – fiendish harbingers of doom with blazing eyes and snarling teeth. The name varies throughout the country – Padfoot in Yorkshire; Gwyllgi in Wales; Moddey Dhoo in the Isle of Man; Trash or Skriker in Lancashire. Whatever their name locally, they are usually referred to nationally as 'Black Shuck', a name derived from the Saxon word *Scucca*, meaning Devil.

Branwell Brontë wrote of these phantoms: 'The Gytrash is a spectre ... [which] mostly appears in the form of some animal; a black dog, dragging a chain, a dusky calf, nay even a rolling stone.' It was an animal such as this that inspired Sir Arthur Conan Doyle to write *The Hound of the Baskervilles*.

Spectral hounds have been reported all over England. One has been seen near Cromer, loping along lanes near Neatishead on the Norfolk Broads and at Wicken Fen, near Newmarket. In Suffolk, people living near Dunwich have reported seeing a ghostly dog at night, the one eye in the centre of its head blazing scarlet or yellow. And it was in that area, during the Second World War, that he gave an American serviceman and his wife a night they would never forget.

196

The couple had rented a flat-topped hut on the edge of Walberswick Marsh, while the husband served at a nearby airbase. One stormy evening they were startled by a violent pounding on the door. The husband peeped through the window and saw a huge black beast battering their home. The terrified couple piled what little furniture they had against the door, then cowered as the attacker hurled his body against first one wall, then another, before leaping onto the roof. The ordeal lasted several hours before the noise faded away. The couple waited anxiously for daylight and at dawn crept outside to inspect the damage. There was no sign of the attack, and no paw or claw marks in the soft mud around the hut.

The West Country is said to have a pack of wild black dogs whose blood-curdling howls have been heard several times across the vast wastes of Dartmoor.

From Haworth and Todmorden in Yorkshire come reports that on All Hallow's Eve out on the high moors, where the reservoirs supply the industrial towns of the north, Hell Hounds rush across the water as easily as over land, only to fade away as they approach the youth hostel at a place called Makinholes.

The beach at Formby on Merseyside has long been reported to be haunted by the fearsome 'Trash', a ghostly black hound whose appearances are echoed by other dogs throughout Britain – a huge black animal with luminous eyes.

In 1962 two staff reporters and a photographer from the *Liverpool Echo* paid a Hallowe'en night visit to Formby beach in search of the ghostly animal. Two of them heard and saw 'a huge, dark shape moving about in clear silhouette atop a nearby sand dune'. Even as they watched, it took on the definite shape of a dog. They moved towards it, and the shape began to move about in circles, much as a dog would.

Hurriedly they climbed the high sand dune, but when they reached the top, there was nothing to be seen, nor were there any footprints or other disturbances of the sand. In their report later they said: 'It is impossible to describe exactly how we felt, in print. Though it might quite easily have been a trick of the imagination, or perhaps even a stray dog, we are sincerely convinced that what we saw and heard was not of this world!'

Mrs Fowler, now living in retirement in Canada, had an interesting experience with a ghostly dog, just after the First World War, at her childhood home in Wigan, Lancashire. She came from a large family of eight girls and four boys and, understandably, the family was quite poor. Because of the size of the family, the eight girls, when they were quite small, slept in one large bed, 'top to tail'.

She told me that one night, when all the girls were in bed, they heard the soft padding of footsteps on the stairs and were surprised when a large black dog came into the room. One of the girls got out of bed and went as if to stroke the dog, but her sisters cautioned her that it might bite. With that, the child climbed back into bed, and the dog went underneath it.

Mrs Fowler said: 'From under the bed, we could hear what appeared to be the dog crunching on a bone. My eldest sister shouted down to father, to ask whether or not he had brought a dog home. Father replied that he had not and told us to go to sleep.'

These visitations became quite frequent, and in the end the girls got used to the dog coming into the bedroom, going under the bed and crunching what sounded like a bone. Each morning, when they got up, there was never a trace of either dog or bone, and the girls were never able to solve the mystery during the time they lived at the house.

Mrs Fowler continued: 'By the time I had reached my teens, our family fortunes had improved and we were able to move into a larger house. The people who moved in after us were a young couple with a small boy. Some months after they moved in, the dog again appeared in the bedroom, which the young boy now occupied, and he, on seeing it, got out of bed to pet the animal. The dog "attacked" him, and he was left in such a terrible condition that he had to spend a long time in Wigan Infirmary.'

Subsequent research has revealed a possible explanation

to these rather weird events. A tenant who lived in the house in the 1890s had been a miserly old man who had no friends and who did not wish to become involved with his neighbours. To enable him to retain some privacy, he had bought himself a big black dog, renowned throughout the neighbourhood for its ferocity. It seems the old man had slept in that bedroom, and each night his guard dog would come upstairs with him, sitting by his bed until the old man gave him a bone. Then both dog and bone would disappear under the bed until morning.

In the 1890s it was a ghostly black dog which saved the life of a Wesleyan preacher who was returning home after making a charitable collection in a rather lonely part of Wensleydale, in North Yorkshire.

As night fell, he found that his route led him through a wood, a mile wide. Knowing that there was no place in the area where he could shelter for the night, the preacher steeled himself and trusted the Almighty to protect him from the dangers of the sinister woods. As he approached the edge of the wood and found a pathway that would lead him through, a large black dog joined him and padded silently ahead of his horse. He was unable to make out where the animal had come from, but it never left him, and when the wood grew so dark that he was unable to see it, he knew by instinct that the animal was still there. When he emerged safely at the other side of the wood, the dog disappeared.

Just then, the preacher realized that he had lost his purse containing all the money he had collected. It must have fallen from his jacket pocket as he made his way through the woods. So, turning his horse round, he set off back into the sinister woods to search for it. At the entrance he was again joined by the strange black dog, which padded beside him; it never touched him and he never spoke to it, but having found the purse he made his way to the edge of the wood again and as he emerged the dog ceased to be there.

This amazing story was given some credence two years later, when two condemned prisoners in York Castle

Prison wrote out their confessions and put on record the fact that they had intended to rob and murder a Wesleyan preacher on that night in the wood, but he had a large black dog with him and when they saw that, they felt that the preacher and the dog together would be too much for them.

A different phantom beast worried hundreds of people in four Devon towns when they woke up on the morning of 6 February 1855. Clearly visible in the heavy overnight snow were animal footprints some four inches long and almost three inches wide – footprints which, it was later discovered, stretched in a zigzag line for nearly one hundred miles, from Topsham, on the River Exe, to Dawlish, and on to Totnes and Torquay.

The footprints, shaped like a hoof, went in a single file, as though some one-legged creature had hopped along, and were exactly 8½ inches apart. Even more amazing was the estimated fact that the prints had covered the hundred miles in four hours. They had crossed the two-mile-wide mouth of the River Exe and passed over rooftops, under and over hedges and up and over hayricks.

If only one person, or the inhabitants of one village, had reported the unexplained 'phantom' steps, the whole thing might have been dismissed as a hoax. But hundreds of people saw them, measured them and drew impressions of them. Inhabitants locked their doors, refusing to go out after dusk, and one enterprising Exeter blacksmith cashed in on the panic with a neat invention – the doorchain – to allow people to open their doors just a few inches to identify callers. Hundreds of these chains were hurriedly made and sold as near-panic gripped the countryside.

Within a week the story was taken up by the newspapers of the day, and soon the story spread throughout the whole country. Then fantastic theories began to pour in – the marks were made by a huge crane, a bird well known in the area at the time, or a badger. However, the Devon folk would have none of that. They insisted then, as now, that the prints were made by a solitary hoof. And what earthly creature could travel a hundred miles on a bitter cold night, over high fences and across rooftops? There was only one answer: these were the marks of the Devil.

A posse of armed men formed a search-party for the 'thing'. But they saw and heard nothing. In fact, the search only increased the people's fear, because it was discovered that the footmarks *started* in the middle of a garden and *ended* in the middle of a field! So the 'thing' had come from nowhere and had gone nowhere. On its journey it had walked through every garden in some hamlets and had never once crossed its own tracks. It had not displaced the snow on either side, walking in a line of single footsteps which could not have been made by man or animal.

In due course the rains came and washed the footprints away. Slowly the tension eased and people went out into the lanes again at night. But the mystery of the phantom footprints has remained unsolved for the past 133 years.

The village of Woolpit on the A45 road, some eight miles east of Bury St Edmunds, was where many servants of the castle at Haughley Park lived. (Haughley Park is now open to the public.) The name of the village derives from Old English and suggests that there was once a lair of wolves in the vicinity. According to local tradition, when snow lies on the ground, a phantom wolf emerges from its long-forgotten lair, lifts its muzzle to the frosty sky – and howls!

The village of Flixton, on the A1039 west of Filey in North Yorkshire goes one better and boasts, of all things, a werewolf, equipped with abnormally large teeth which glow in the dark, and it exudes a ghastly stench 'like rotting corpses'. Its eyes are crimson and dart fire, while its tail is almost as long as its body, capable of felling any nocturnal wayfarer it might meet.

There is substantial historical evidence to suggest how the tradition came about, for history books tell us that in about AD 940 a hostel was built at Flixton, specifically to shelter wayfarers in winter time, from attacks from wolves. In those days it was not uncommon for packs of the animals to roam those parts, and they were regarded with loathing, because in times of very severe weather conditions they scavenged the graveyards. Their cunning in discovering unprotected cattle, their boldness in attacking travellers, plus their habit of suddenly descending in large numbers on an area where they had previously been unknown, all helped to give rise to the belief that the animals were not ordinary wolves but human beings who adopted a wolf-like shape at night.

Modern medical science has since shown that this was not as far-fetched as it may sound, for at one time there may well have been a member of the community who suffered from lycanthropy a rare but real disease. The affected person, if left untreated by modern drugs, will behave in exactly the same way as a wolf, even to the extent of moving about on all fours and gnawing raw meat. It would not have needed much for traveller's tales of attacks by wolves, plus a case of lycanthropy in the area, to become distorted in the re-telling and acquire some supernatural touches.

Drive along the B1052 from Newmarket to Saffron Walden in Essex, and your headlights may momentarily illuminate an animal which could persuade you that there is a zoo in the area. You would be wrong, of course, for what you saw would have been the phantom known locally as 'the Shug monkey'. It haunts the stretch of road and the lanes between West Wratting and Balsham, having the body of a large black shaggy sheepdog and the face of a monkey. Sometimes it has been seen walking erect, and at others loping on all fours at supernatural speed in the gloom.

Between Etruria and Handley in Staffordshire, a ghostly white rabbit has been seen, which is said to jump out from one side of the road and run along the path for a short while before disappearing. It always takes the same route and disappears at a spot called The Grove.

Another spectral white rabbit has been seen by a number of people in the Kidsgrove area. Occasionally it has been seen crossing the avenue leading to Clough Hall, and its appearance is said to predict a forthcoming death.

One man who saw the animal, just before the Second World War, said that three days after the incident his father died. Others speak of seeing the rabbit and then relations or close friends have died suddenly within a very short time.

The milltown of Rochdale in Lancashire has a ghostly bunny, known locally as 'the Baum Rabbit', whose legend goes back to the mid-eighteenth century, when St Mary's Church was founded and the graveyard opened. The churchyard soon became known as 'the Baum', which is derived from an old Lancashire term for a herb which grew there and which was used throughout the area as a cure for anything from boils to bed-wetting.

Some years ago, a ghostly rabbit used to visit the churchyard. It was a healthy-looking animal, lively and plump enough to last a family for two meals, which suggests that the churchyard herbs agreed with it. The rabbit was said to be whiter than the driven snow, always beautiful and clean and always seen rummaging among the churchyard rubbish, as if in search of something. No one was able to get very close to it though, for the slightest sound or movement caused it to disappear into thin air.

Tradition has it that many years ago some foul deed was perpetrated on that spot and as a result the rabbit was doomed to haunt the area. The truth of the matter is lost in the mists of time, but it is on record that the phantom white rabbit has frightened a number of local residents over the years.

In the late nineteenth century, the villagers around Crank and Rainford, near St Helens in Merseyside, lived in fear of spotting 'the White Rabbit of Crank', a ghostly rabbit described in contemporary accounts as being large and with big floppy ears. It was said to jump out at travellers and hop alongside them. Again, several people are said to have died in mysterious circumstances after encountering it, and those who lived to tell the tale knew that their sighting was an indication of approaching trouble. When the railway line was built to Rainford Junction, it was assumed that the trains would scare the ghostly rodent away, but people still insist that the White Rabbit of Crank can be glimpsed occasionally on dark nights – and those who see it can be assured that ill-fortune lies ahead!

Spectral cats seem to be amongst the most familiar phantoms. Just why this should be, no one seems to know, but they are the most common form of phenomena. The tradition of ghostly cats goes back to the time of the ancient Egyptians, who worshipped them as gods, and across the centuries tradition has asserted that the Devil himself can assume the guise of a friendly old cat.

It was the author Christina Hole who said that, 'No one who has ever loved a cat can possibly believe that faithful friend to be a mere soulless creature that lives for a few years and then dies forever.' Perhaps the fact that there are manifestations of deceased people means some kind of life after death for human beings, and happily the same proof is available with regard to a future life for animals. Cats are supposed to have nine lives, but there seem to be a lot of people who reckon they have a tenth – people who are convinced they have seen cat ghosts, such as that of Stripey.

Stripey was a beautiful ginger cat who was hit by a car as she crossed the road, and died a few days later. Several years after she died, one of the family, who had been a schoolgirl at the time of Stripey's accident, was sitting quietly in the living-room, reading. Looking up from her book, she saw Stripey basking in a pool of sunlight at the end of the settee, contentedly washing her face. It all seemed so natural that it was a minute or two before she realized that Stripey was dead and buried in the garden. She glanced up again, but the cat was gone – there was nothing but a pool of sunlight on the carpet.

Mrs Gladys Golden and her family moved to Barrow-in-Furness from Birmingham in 1975, and before very long she was mystified by the appearance, over a period of several weeks, of a big black-and-white cat. She told me: 'One day I was making my daughter's bed when I thought

I saw a big black-and-white cat run into the bedroom and dash under the bed. Thinking it was our cat, who was not allowed upstairs, I shouted and "shooed", and when I looked under the bed, it seemed to have gone. However, to be on the safe side I checked the bathroom and the other bedroom. There was no sign of it.'

. Following this, Mrs Golden went downstairs and was surprised to find her own cat asleep on the hearthrug. She was even more surprised when she realized that the living-room door had been shut all the time and there was no possible way for her own cat to have got upstairs.

Some time later, Mrs Golden's daughter Linda came from Birmingham to stay for a week. Linda and her younger sister, Christine, who was still living at home, decided they would sleep together downstairs on the bed settee. As they were making it up, both Linda and her mother became aware of the loud purring of a contented cat, although Christine heard nothing. Mrs Golden continued: 'I went through into the kitchen, where I discovered my own cat was asleep in his basket. The purring Linda and I heard appeared to have been coming from the rug in front of the fire!'

Next morning, Linda said that she had been unable to sleep for most of the night, on account of the loud purring of the mysterious phantom cat. Later that same morning, the milkman called for his money. Mrs Golden said: 'As I paid him, the same big black-and-white cat ran up the stairs. I said to the milkman, "Did you see that cat run upstairs?" He said he had not noticed it, but Linda, who had followed me out into the hall, said, "I saw it, Mum!"'

Cats, it must be remembered, are creatures of great habit. They have their favourite places – mine prefers my antique rocking-chair to any other – and they will always return to them, even from beyond the grave. Perhaps this can best be illustrated by the experiences of Miss D. Cullen of Canterbury, who said: 'My cat adopted me when she was about eleven years old. When she came, she was full of grief, but she soon became joyful and interested in everything I did, shouting her welcome when I came into the house. By the time she was seventeen, she was beginning to show her age. She was not at all well and the vet diagnosed kidney trouble. This deteriorated and reluctantly I had to consent to her being put to sleep, and this was done in the evening.'

The following morning, the cat walked into Miss Cullen's bedroom. She continued: 'I saw her quite clearly and heard her loud "good morning" shout. I heard her for several nights after this, jumping on and off her favourite chair and getting a drink of water. About a week later, I heard her and felt her curl up on the bed at my feet, but this time I could not see her. I have often felt her place her chin, as she always did, with some pressure, on my arm,' she concluded.

A pet cat belonging to an elderly lady who lived in an isolated house in Cheshire was found dead one winter evening, lying near the garage. It was her well-loved tortoiseshell, Thomas. The lady and her husband had thought the world of Thomas and were quite naturally upset at his sudden demise. Her husband gently wrapped the cat in cloth and, despite the fact that it was beginning to snow, took him into the garden and buried him under a small tree, where for hours at a time during the summer months the cat used to sit or sleep.

One of the cat's more endearing habits had been to jump onto the window-sill and, reaching out with his paw, rattle the door latch when he wanted to come in. A couple of evenings after the cat's death, the woman was alone in the house and was surprised to hear the latch rattling on the back door. On checking, she was amazed to see it gently moving up and down – just as it used to when Thomas was alive. She told her husband of the incident when he returned home later that evening, but he didn't believe her and said she was imagining things.

The same thing happened again a few nights later, and she told me she thought it was her husband, who was not known for his sensitivity, playing tricks on her. She said: 'I had the last laugh though, for the next night we were both at home when it happened again, and my husband saw the latch move too. He dashed to the door and opened it, but there was no one there – except for an imprint of a cat's paws on the window-sill in the fresh snow. No prints were found, either on the step or on the path, just on the window-sill!'

Her husband, who has since died, never laughed at her again, and she said that she found some consolation in the belief that cats, too, can live on after their death.

One morning in the autumn of 1976, lorry-driver Barry Mason, who lived in a modern council house in Tamworth, Staffordshire, had left home for work, and his wife, Margaret, was having an extra half-hour in bed. Mrs Mason later told reporters: 'I was just lying there dozing. Suddenly I felt a cat jump on the bed and walk softly around looking for a comfortable spot to settle itself on the eiderdown.'

She thought it was Puss, the family's long-haired tabby, and got up to look for it. She looked under the bed, everywhere, but there was no sign of it. The door and window were both shut and she supposed she must have been imagining things. A couple of days later, the same thing happened again, exactly in the same way, and again two days after that. 'That was when I decided to tackle my husband about it,' said Mrs Mason. 'He said, "Don't be silly. The cat isn't in. I always put him out after I've fed him."

'Two mornings later, there it was again. I could even feel its paw on my shoulder, and I don't know why but I went cold all over and began to shiver. I felt the cat slowly sinking into the eiderdown and curl up.'

Although Mr and Mrs Mason had not seen the cat, they felt sure that their three-year-old son, Mark, had seen it, because one day he told Mrs Mason's mother, 'Granny, me got two pussies.' It seems that the Masons' cat had also seen it, and he didn't like it. Mrs Mason said: 'Puss refused to come into the house, and we had to catch him and bring him in to feed him. Then he would become violent if we didn't let him out again immediately afterwards. He would go all weird, staring round and growling, his fur sticking up.'

Then, in January 1977, Mrs Mason's previously sceptical husband came face to face with the phantom cat. He said: 'I was sitting drinking a cup of coffee when this black cat walked across the living-room floor and went behind the settee. I went to get it to put it outside, but as I bent to pick it up – it simply vanished through the wall!' Now the family were convinced they had a phantom black cat which they eventually grew to accept and which Mrs Mason said she found soothing. 'After all,' she concluded, 'it kept away the phantom mice!'

Although most phantom cats seem to be friendly enough, as a child Mrs E. Nelson of Cleethorpes had a real scare when her cat, Tiddles, returned from the dead.

She said that one night she was wakened by a loud purring and the feeling of something pulling at her bedclothes. She sat up, thinking that her cat, which had disappeared several months before, had come home, but she was unable to find him, although she felt all over the bed. Thinking she had been dreaming, she lay down again and immediately the purring and clawing began once more. Thoroughly frightened, she pulled the bedclothes over her head, but the cat, purring louder, pulled so fiercely on them that she had to hold on tight to the sheets.

She said: 'I shouted for my mother, but she couldn't hear me as I was under the bedclothes.' Shortly the cat stopped, but Mrs Nelson was too afraid to look and just lay terrified until morning, waiting for her mother to wake up. When her mother did wake, the girl told her to come in as there was a cat in the bedroom. Her mother came running, but there was no cat, nor any way one could have got into the room. But there, on the sheets, were several dirty paw-marks!

Early this century, Laburnham Villa at Hoe Benham, a small village near Newbury, was owned by the artists Pittman and Waud. One morning in November 1907 they were painting in their garden studio, waiting for the arrival of a friend and fellow artist, Miss Clarissa Miles, who lived nearby. About ten o'clock Oswald Pittman went up to the cottage and, looking along the lane that led to the house, he saw Miss Miles approaching, carrying an easel and palette and, much to his surprise, accompanied by a very large white pig with an abnormally long snout. He thought, rather sourly, 'I hope she leaves that outside and closes the gate. We don't want a pig wandering over the garden.'

When Miss Miles arrived a few minutes later, she was alone and was rather taken aback when she heard what Pittman had seen, for she said that, if she had not actually seen the creature, surely she would have heard its grunting and pattering. However, Pittman was adamant that she had walked up the lane accompanied by a pig – a large white one – and both he and Miss Miles retraced her steps to the village to search for the animal but found nothing.

Children who had been playing in the lane as she passed said they had seen no pig, and the following morning the milkman, who had been in the lane at the time, swore that he had seen no pig either and that the whole area was under a swine-fever order anyway, so any straying livestock were liable to be destroyed.

This was only one of many sightings of the mysterious ghostly pig of Hoe Benham. As far back as 1850, seven or eight men, returning on a hay waggon, were approaching King's Farm when the horses suddenly went wild. Every man on the waggon saw a white shape floating round the horses, until it eventually floated across the lane and into a field, before vanishing.

At the same spot, in 1873, a man called Barratt saw, in broad daylight, a creature which he said resembled a giant sheep. It was pawing at the ground in the middle of the road and when Barratt hit out at it with his stick, the apparition vanished before the blow struck it. In the autumn of 1904, Mr Albert Thorne reported that he had heard a buzzing noise and saw something 'like a calf knuckled down'. The animal was, according to his estimation, some 2½ feet high and five feet long, with glowing eyes. Although Mr Thorne never took his eyes off it for one moment, the creature gradually faded from sight. Another witness said that on a bright moonlit night in the winter of 1905 he saw a large animal, which he assumed was the curate's dog, near the gates of Laburnham Villa. He was about to grab it and return it to its owner, when it seemed to turn into a large pig which reared on its hind legs before vanishing.

Just east of Aylesbury, on the borders of Buckinghamshire and Hertfordshire and reached from Tring by the A41, is a stretch of unspoiled English countryside. Most of the area belongs to the Forestry Commission, protected as an area of outstanding beauty.

Drive along the A41 through the hamlet of St Leonards, pass the enclosed Uphill reservoir and you will arrive at the lovely village of Cholesbury, once an important hill fort in the Iron Age, which covered some fourteen or fifteen acres. A couple of thousand years ago some abnormal occurrences here gave rise to what is considered to be one of the most peculiar hauntings in the south of England.

During the hours of darkness, the district is often disturbed by eerie screams, grunts and roars of a mass of animals. This weird phenomenon is usually heard on cloudy, moonless nights, which makes the animals difficult to see. However, those who have seen them say that they look like small black pigs which, apart from goring and biting, appear to be trying to burrow into the ground.

Several plausible theories have been put forward to account for the mysterious animals: badgers, foxes or even a rare species of deer which are believed to have escaped from Woburn Abbey Park. However, apart from the fact that these creatures are either gentle or live solitary lives, never moving in packs, examination of the damp ground on which the animals have been seen and heard fighting shows no trace of hoofprints or any other disturbance.

No one really knows where the ghostly screaming pigs come from, or why, but the suggestion is that some prehistoric carnage took place outside the walls of the Iron Age fort – and this is the motivation for the screaming pigs of Cholesbury!

Index

Index